Losing The Thread

Also by Alie Stibbe:

Books

Frayed at the Edges: Wit and wisdom for women in mid-life and beyond
   (Monarch, Oxford, in preparation)
A Spacious Place (BRF: Oxford, in preparation)
All Stitched Up: Wit and wisdom for today's woman (Monarch: Oxford, 2005)
Barefoot in the Kitchen: Bible readings and reflections for mothers (BRF:
   Oxford, 2004)
Bursting at the Seams: A wealth of wit and wisdom, for, by and about women
   (co-compiled with Killy John, Monarch: Oxford, 2004)

Translations

The Final Conflict – Defenders of the Sign Part 3, by Kristian Kapelrud,
   translated by Alie Stibbe (Piquant Press, in preparation)
The Pact – Defenders of the Sign Part 2, by Kristian Kapelrud, translated by
   Alie Stibbe (Piquant Press, in preparation)
The Sign – Defenders of the Sign Part 1, by Kristian Kapelrud, translated by
   Alie Stibbe (Piquant Press, in preparation)
Word Bytes: The Completely Manageable Bible, by Knut Tveitereid, translated
   by Alie Stibbe (BRF: Oxford, 2003)

Note to church magazine editors

Losing The Thread

Joyful wit and wisdom for today's woman

Compiled by
Alie Stibbe

MONARCH
BOOKS

Oxford, UK & Grand Rapids, Michigan, USA

First published in the UK in 2009 by Monarch Books
(a publishing imprint of Lion Hudson plc),
Wilkinson House, Jordan Hill Road, Oxford OX2 8DR.
Tel: +44 (0)1865 302750 Fax: +44 (0)1865 302757
Email: monarch@lionhudson.com
www.lionhudson.com

ISBN: 978-1-85424-907-4 (UK)
ISBN: 978-0-8254-6310-5 (USA)

Distributed by:
UK: Marston Book Services Ltd, PO Box 269,
Abingdon, Oxon OX14 4YN;
USA: Kregel Publications, PO Box 2607, Grand Rapids,
Michigan 49501

Illustrations by Darren Harvey-Regan

Preface

Five years ago I came across a quote by Elaine Gill: 'If you have any doubts that we live in a society controlled by men, try reading down the index of contributors to a volume of quotations, looking for women's names.' I was not necessarily concerned as to which sex ultimately controlled society, but, in my growing interest in determining what women had to say – if anything at all – I decided to test Elaine's premise. In the 40,000 word manuscript of wit and wisdom my husband had then co-compiled, I found only five entries attributed to women. A similar situation became apparent in other collections I examined, even in those compiled by women.

Bursting at the Seams was the result of trying to rectify this trend. My co-compiler and I scoured the media for women who had made quotable sayings about topics we felt were relevant to women's issues. We did include some quotes by men – but not many! It was a fascinating first foray into the world of women's words: and I was hooked.

As an author's output tends to reflect their stage in life, *Bursting at the Seams* reflected my emergence from the mothering of young children and my surprise at having some time on my hands when they started school. My second compilation, *All Stitched Up*, took the exercise a step further. By this time I had returned to higher education and was pursuing a Masters degree. The quotes in that volume were purely by women and the topics deeper and more edgy – reflecting that more adventurous stage in my philosophical explorations.

This third volume, *Losing the Thread*, comes hot on the heels of my return to professional life, but at a stage when everything around me is changing and the nest is beginning to empty. Just as I thought I had life 'all stitched up', like many women my age I find I am 'losing the thread' – asking deep questions about life as a radical new chapter opens before me, and looking for significant answers that will form the foundation of the 'deeper wisdom' that women are supposed to accede to in their later years! I feel that the topics and the quotations in this volume reflect the beginnings of that quest.

I hope that those of you who enjoyed my previous compilations will laugh, reflect and grow with me through my choice of wit and wisdom in this new volume, for, in the words of Joyce Carol Oates: *It is only through disruptions and confusion that we grow, jarred out of ourselves by the collision of someone else's private world with our own.* Through this compilation I offer you a small collision with my private world, but I hope it is not purely jarring, but also somewhat joyful. Have fun!

Alie Stibbe
April 2009

A

Achievement

Achievement brings its own anticlimax.

Agatha Christie

Great things are only possible with outrageous requests.

Thea Alexander

Where I was born and where and how I have lived is unimportant. It is what I have done with where I have been that should be of interest.

Georgia O'Keeffe

The whole point of getting things done is knowing what to leave undone.

Lady Stella Reading

Measure not the work, until the day's out and the labour done.

Elizabeth Barrett Browning

Every achievement, big or small, begins in your mind.

Mary Kay Ash

The Ladder of Achievement

The likelihood of your achieving a task is directly related to your attitude... If you don't like your score...what are you going to do about your attitude?

100%	I did it
90%	I will
80%	I can
70%	I think I can
60%	I might
50%	I think I might
40%	What is it?
30%	I wish I could
20%	I don't know how
10%	I can't
0%	I won't

Author unknown

Out of the strain of doing...
and into the peace of the done.

Julia Woodruff

Action

The time when you need to do something is when no one else is willing to do it, when people are saying it can't be done.

Mary Frances Berry

Remember, people will judge you by your actions, not your intentions. You may have a heart of gold – but so does a hard-boiled egg.

Anonymous

Action indeed is the sole medium of expression for ethics.

Jane Addams

Doing is a quantum leap from imagining. Thinking about swimming isn't much like actually getting in the water.

Barbara Sher

Trust in God –
and do something.

Mary Lyon

To act and act wisely when the time for action comes, to wait and wait patiently when it is time for repose, will put man in accord with the rising and falling tides, so that with nature and law at his back, and truth and beneficence as his beacon light, he may accomplish wonders.

Helena Petrova Blavatsky

It is time to apply in the arena of the world the wisdom and experience that women have gained over so many thousands of years.

Aung San Suu Kyi

It's not so much how busy you are, but why you are busy. The bee is praised. The mosquito is swatted.

Mary O'Connor

Advice

I sometimes give myself admirable advice, but I am incapable of taking it.

Lady Mary Wortley Montagu

Advice is one of those things it is far more blessed to give than to receive.

Carolyn Wells

Strange, when you ask anyone's advice you see yourself what is right.

Selma Lagerlof

The strongest possible piece of advice I would give any young woman is:
Don't screw around, and don't smoke.

Edwina Currie

I am very handy with my advice and then when anybody appears to be following it, I get frantic.

Flannery O'Connor

A woman in love never takes advice.

Rosamond Marshall

Study as if you were going to live forever; live as if you were going to die tomorrow.

Maria Mitchell

People are always willing to follow advice when it accords with their own wishes.

Lady Blessington

My mother gave me some smart advice – you can do and be anything if you're willing to deal with how other people respond to you. I was willing to take whatever anybody would dish out for the right to be myself.

Whoopi Goldberg

> It is very difficult to live among people you love and hold back from offering advice.
>
> *Anne Tyler*

As time passes we all get better at blazing a trail through the thicket of advice.

Margot Bennett

Age

Being young is beautiful, but being old is comfortable.

Author unknown

I used to dread getting older because I thought I would not be able to do all the things I wanted to do, but now that I am older I find that I don't want to do them.

Nancy Astor

We did not change as we grew older; we just became more clearly ourselves.

Lynn Hall

> Inside every older woman is a young girl wondering what the hell happened.
>
> *Cora Harvey Armstrong*

You can't kid yourself when you're in your seventies. You have to do the things you want to do because there is no more rehearsal time left.

Joan Burstein
'I feel like I'm in my prime', You,
7 December 2003

The older we get, the younger old is.

Meg Ivan

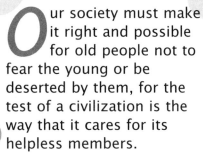

Our society must make it right and possible for old people not to fear the young or be deserted by them, for the test of a civilization is the way that it cares for its helpless members.

Pearl S. Buck

Age has extremely little to do with anything that matters. The difference between one age and another is, as a rule, enormously exaggerated.

Rose McCaulay

We turn not older with years, but newer every day.

Emily Dickinson

Of all the self-fulfilling prophecies in our culture, the assumption that aging means decline and poor health is probably the deadliest.

Marilyn Ferguson

I refuse to admit that I am more than 52, even if that makes my children illegitimate.

Nancy Astor

I feel that every year I grow older I become more beautiful. It's about being comfortable with age and loving those little lines. In youth, I didn't have wisdom and now in my mid-thirties I feel that I have it all.

Kelly Lurchford

You can't turn back the clock; but you can wind it up again.

Bonnie Prudden

> ## Old age is no place for sissies.
> *Bette Davis*

The older I get the greater power I seem to have to help the world; I am like a snowball…the further I am rolled the more I gain.

Susan B Anthony

> ## It is not how old you are, but how you are old.
> *Marie Dressler*

I've decided that now is the time to do all the daft things I was far too sensible and self-conscious to do in my youth.

Esther Rantzen

> Now that I'm over sixty, I'm veering toward respectability.
>
> *Shelley Winters*

Anger

> nger is not bad. Anger can be a very positive thing, the thing that moves us beyond the acceptance of evil.
>
> *Joan Chittister*

 If you are patient in one moment of anger, you will escape a hundred days of sorrow.

Chinese proverb

The more anger towards the past you carry in your heart, the less capable you are of loving in the present.

Barbara De Angelis

> I am angry nearly every day of my life, but I have learned not to show it; and I still try to hope not to feel it, though it may take me another forty years to do it.
>
> *Louisa May Alcott*

He who angers you conquers you.

Elizabeth Kenny

The best remedy for a short
temper is a long walk.
Jacqueline Schiff

Ambition

Instead of thinking about where you are, think about where you want to be. It takes twenty years of hard work to become an overnight success.

Diana Rankin

A man without ambition is dead. A man with ambition but no love is dead. A man with ambition and love for his blessings here on earth is ever so alive. Having been alive, it won't be so hard in the end to lie down and rest.

Pearl Bailey

Reach for the stars, even if you have to stand on a cactus.

Susan Longacre

An aim in life is the only fortune worth finding.

Jacqueline Kennedy Onassis

Give yourself something to work toward – constantly.

Mary Kay Ash

Very few people are ambitious in the sense of having a specific image of what they want to achieve. Most people's sights are only toward the next rung, the next increment of money.

Judith M. Bardwick

I have been absolutely hag-ridden with ambition. If I could wish to have anything in the world it would be to be free of ambition.

Tallulah Bankhead

It seems to me we can never give up longing and wishing while we are thoroughly alive. There are certain things we feel to be beautiful and good, and we must hunger after them.

George Eliot

If you have a great ambition, take as big a step as possible in the direction of fulfilling it. The step may only be a tiny one, but trust that it may be the largest one possible for now.

Mildred Mcafee

Ambition if it feeds at all, does so on the ambition of others.

Susan Sontag

Apology

An apology is the superglue of life. It can repair just about anything.

Lynn Johnston

If love means never having to say you're sorry, then marriage means always having to say everything twice.

Estelle Getty

An apology is a good way to have the last word.

Author unknown

True remorse is never just a regret over consequence; it is a regret over motive.

Mignon McLaughlin

Apology is a lovely perfume; it can transform the clumsiest moment into a gracious gift.

Margaret Lee Runbeck

Repentance should be more than saying sorry. It requires a change of both words and actions.

Tamsin Ormond

It's terribly important to be honest about your motivation – an apology that lacks regret can do more harm than good.

Sally Brampton

Appearance

A half century of living should put a good deal into a woman's face besides some wrinkles and some unwelcome folds around the chin.

Frances Parkinson Keyes

The best cosmetic in the world is an active mind that is always finding something new.

Mary Meek Atkeson

I've never been interested in fashion or looks. The truth is that all I really require of a hairstyle is that I can see to drive the car.

Sandi Toksvig

I never go out unless I look like Joan Crawford the movie star. If you want to see the girl next door, go next door.

Joan Crawford

Appearances are not held to be a clue to the truth. But we seem to have no other.

Ivy Compton-Burnett

We all lose our looks eventually. Better develop your character and interest in life.

Jacqueline Bisset

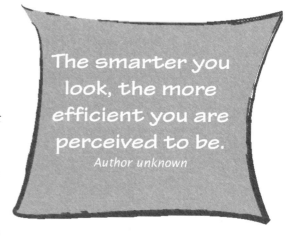

The smarter you look, the more efficient you are perceived to be.

Author unknown

My appearance has changed a lot over the years, but it has far more to do with how I feel about being a woman.

Emma Thompson

My husband said he wanted to have a relationship with a redhead, so I dyed my hair.

Jane Fonda

Nature often holds up a mirror so we can see more clearly the ongoing processes of growth, renewal and transformation in our lives.

Mary Ann Brussat

Even I don't wake up looking like Cindy Crawford.

Cindy Crawford

Approval & Appreciation

Those whose approval you seek most give you the least.

Rozanne Weissman

A compliment is a gift, not to be thrown away carelessly, unless you want to hurt the giver.

Eleanor Hamilton

No one ever told me I was pretty when I was a little girl. All little girls should be told they're pretty, even if they aren't.

Marilyn Monroe

Twice in your life are you approved by everyone: When you learn to walk and when you learn to read.

Penelope Fitzgerald

Appreciation can make a day...even change a life.
Your willingness to put it into words is all that is necessary.
Margaret Cousins

The more one does and sees and feels, the more one is able to do, and the more genuine may be one's appreciation of fundamental things like home, and love, and understanding companionship.
Amelia Earhart

Look at everything as though you were seeing it either for the first or last time.
Betty Smith

Like when I'm in the bathroom looking at my toilet paper, I'm like 'Wow! That's toilet paper?' I don't know if we appreciate how much we have.
Alicia Silverstone

Assertiveness

Assertiveness helps us keep our balance. Because the assertive woman accepts herself as she is, she finds it easier to accept others as they are, with all their faults and foibles.

Michelle Guinness

We have to find a way of standing up for ourselves without becoming shrill and aggressively defensive, and without thinking we have to destroy a man in entering a fight with him.

Claire Foster

The basic difference between being assertive and being aggressive is how our words and behaviour affect the rights and well being of others.

Sharon Anthony Bower

Never allow a person to tell you 'no' who doesn't have the power to say 'yes'.

Eleanor Roosevelt

Attitude

Just because you're miserable doesn't mean you can't enjoy your life.

Annette Goodheart

Happiness is an attitude. We either make ourselves miserable, or happy and strong. The amount of work is the same.

Francesca Reigler

It's so hard when I have to, and so easy when I want to.

Annie Gottlier

If you don't like something, change it; if you can't change it, change the way you think about it.

Mary Engelbreit

We plant seeds that will flower as results in our lives, so best to remove the weeds of anger, avarice, envy and doubt...

Dorothy Day

You find yourself refreshed in the presence of cheerful people. Why not make an honest effort to confer that pleasure on others? Half the battle is gained if you never allow yourself to say anything gloomy.

Lydia M. Child

I like trees because they seem more resigned to the way they have to live than other things do.

Willa Cather

Bite off more than you can chew, then chew it.

Ella Williams

You control your attitude
or it controls you.

Anon

Say you are well, or all is well
with you, and God shall hear
your words and make them true.

Ella Wheeler Wilcox

I am convinced that attitude is the key to success or failure in almost any of life's endeavours. Your attitude – your perspective, your outlook, how you feel about yourself, how you feel about other people – determines your priorities, your actions, your values. Your attitude determines how you interact with other people and how you interact with yourself.

Caroline Warner

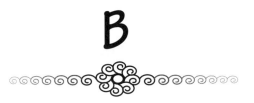

B

Babies

When babies look beyond you and giggle,
maybe they're seeing angels.

Eileen Elias Freeman

It was the tiniest thing I ever decided to put my whole life into.

Terri Guillemets

I don't dislike babies, though I think very young ones rather disgusting.

Queen Victoria

It sometimes happens, even in the best of families, that a baby is born. This is not necessarily cause for alarm. The important thing is to keep your wits about you and borrow some money.

Elinor Goulding Smith

A baby is a blank cheque made payable to the human race.

Barbara Christine Seifert

A baby is an angel whose wings decrease as his legs increase.

Author unknown

An ugly baby is a very nasty object, and the prettiest is frightful when undressed.

Queen Victoria

Whenever I held my newborn baby in my arms, I used to think that what I said and did to him could have an influence not only on him but on all whom he met, not only for a day or a month or a year, but for all eternity – a very challenging and exciting thought for a mother.

Rose Kennedy

Beauty

Beauty... is the shadow of God on the universe.

Gabriela Mistral

Most of us can't be beautiful, but who cares?

Esther Rantzen

What is beautiful is good, and who is good will soon be beautiful.

Sappho

Beauty comes in all sizes, not just size 10.

Roseanne

Plain women know more about men than beautiful ones do. But beautiful women don't need to know about men. It's the men who have to know about beautiful women.

Katharine Hepburn

How goodness heightens beauty.

Hannah More

We find beautiful those physical characteristics that suggest nubility, fecundity, health and good design.

Nancy Etcoff

To cultivate the sense of the beautiful is one of the most effectual ways of cultivating an appreciation of the divine goodness.

Margaret Thatcher

Bed

I have always felt that the moment when you wake up in the morning is the most wonderful of the twenty-four hours. No matter how weary or dreary you may feel, you possess the certainty... absolutely anything may happen.
Monica Baldwin

No one ever died from sleeping in an unmade bed.
Erma Bombeck

Put duties aside at least an hour before bed, and perform soothing, quiet activities that will help you relax.
Dianne Hales

Sleeping in a bed – it is, apparently, of immense importance. Against those who sleep, from choice or necessity, elsewhere society feels righteously hostile. It is not done. It is disorderly, anarchical.
Rose Macaulay

Bed is the best place for reading, thinking, or doing nothing.
Doris Lessing

No matter how big or soft or warm your bed is, you still have to get out of it.
Grace Slick

It's very difficult to be married to somebody and write books.
When you're married, you can't read in bed,
you can't write at all hours, you can't chase around.
Pauline Kael

Behaviour

Good manners have much to do with the emotions. To make them ring true, one must feel them, not merely exhibit them.

Amy Vanderbilt

The modern rule is that every woman should be her own chaperon.

Amy Vanderbilt

Manners are a sensitive awareness of the feelings of others. If you have that awareness, you have good manners, no matter what fork you use.

Emily Post

I place a high moral value on the way people behave. I find it repellent to have a lot, and to behave with anything other than courtesy in the old sense of the word – politeness of the heart, a gentleness of the spirit.

Emma Thompson

If we stick to good manners and good behaviour, we're released from having to think too much.

Elizabeth Buchan

To be a successful hostess, when guests arrive say, 'At last!' and when they leave say, 'So soon!'

Author unknown

Our humility rests upon a series of learned behaviours, woven together into patterns that are infinitely fragile and never directly inherited.

Margaret Mead

Blame

In passing, also, I would like to say that the first time Adam had a chance he laid the blame on a woman.

Nancy Astor

Let us look at our own faults, and not other people's. We ought not to insist on everyone following in our footsteps, or to take upon ourselves to give instructions in spirituality when, perhaps, we do not even know what it is.

Saint Theresa of Lisieux

We all participate in weaving the social fabric; we should therefore all participate in patching the fabric when it develops holes.

Anne C. Weisberg

I praise loudly. I blame softly.

Catherine II of Russia

Placing the blame or judgment on someone else leaves you powerless to change your experience. Taking responsibility for your beliefs and judgments gives you the power to change them.

Byron Katie

Body

The body never lies.
Martha Graham

**Emotion always has its roots in the unconscious
and manifests itself in the body.**
Irene Claremont de Castillejo

Flesh goes on pleasuring us, and humiliating us, right to the end.
Mignon McLaughlin

_Yet this is health: To have a body functioning so perfectly that when its few
simple needs are met it never calls attention to its own existence._
Bertha Stuart Dyment

I think plastic surgery is like tattoos. If you're happy with the results,
you push the button again and again. A lot of women go too far.
It's easy to fall into that trap and you can begin to look really scary.
There has to be a point where you have to stop...
Sharon Osbourne

I have flabby thighs, but fortunately my stomach covers them.
Joan Rivers

The body is a sacred garment.
Martha Graham

I believe that the physical is the geography of being.
Louise Nevelson

Over the years our bodies become walking autobiographies, telling friends and strangers alike of the minor and major stresses of our lives.

Marilyn Ferguson

The body says what words cannot.

Martha Graham

We should be provided with a new body about the age of thirty or so when we have learnt to attend to it with consideration.

Freya Stark

You have to have the kind of body that doesn't need a girdle in order to get to pose in one.

Carolyn Kenmore

Our bodies are shaped to bear children, and our lives are a working out of the processes of creation. All our ambitions and intelligence are beside that great elemental point.

Phyllis Mcginley

Books

Books are the shoes with which we tread the footsteps of great minds.

Author unknown

Books are the carriers of civilization. Without books, history is silent, literature dumb, science crippled, thought and speculation at a standstill. They are engines of change, windows on the world, lighthouses erected in the sea of time.

Barbara W. Tuchman

Books... are like lobster shells, we surround ourselves with them; then we grow out of them and leave them behind, as evidence of our earlier stages of development.

Dorothy L. Sayers

Anyone who says they have only one life to live must not know how to read a book.

Author unknown

We are made whole by books, as by great space and the stars.

Mary Carolyn Davies

Trusting children and books is a revolutionary act.
Books are, after all, dangerous stuff. Leave a child alone
with a book and you don't know what might happen.
Susan Ohanian

When they ask me at the Post Office if my package contains anything
dangerous, I never know quite how to answer. It contains books, and if a book
isn't dangerous, then why was it written?
Karen Oberst

No man can be called friendless who has God
and the companionship of good books.
Elizabeth Barrett Browning

Boredom

I have done my part to stamp out
boredom in certain quarters of this
world where it threatened to become
rampant. If I accomplish little else, I
shall consider my life justified by that
one fact. Down with boredom.
Elsa Maxwell

The cure for boredom
is curiosity. There is
no cure for curiosity.
Ellen Parr

What makes life dreary
is the want of a motive.
George Eliot

Boredom is like a
pitiless zooming in on
the epidermis of time.
Every instant is dilated and
magnified like the pores of
the face.

Charlotte Whitton

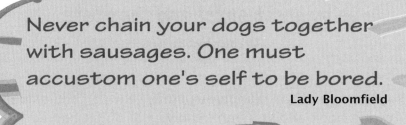

Never chain your dogs together with sausages. One must accustom one's self to be bored.

Lady Bloomfield

Right now, things are so frantic, every minute is filled with activities or planning activities and everything else that goes in between: I'd love to be bored.

Donna Haines

If you always do what interests you, at least one person is pleased.

Katharine Hepburn

There are days when any electrical appliance in the house, including the vacuum cleaner, offers more entertainment than the TV set.

Harriet Van Horne

Boredom is just the reverse side of fascination: both depend on being outside rather than inside a situation, and one leads to the other.

Susan Sontag

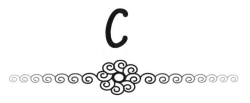

Career

Do the right thing and the money will come.
Gun Denhart

There just aren't enough blonde women in business...
Martha Lane Fox

If you spend money on it – it's a hobby.
If you make money on it – it's a business.
Author unknown

**Sometimes you wonder how you got on this mountain.
But sometimes you wonder, How will I get off?**
Joan Manley

*I've never thought in terms of a traditional career.
I think of a professional life as one pearl added to the next,
making a beautiful necklace you can look at in the end.*
Sharon Patrick

There's plenty of room at the top, but
there's no room to sit down.
Helen Downey

The easiest way for a woman to become a top executive is to buy the company.
Marion Sandler

We have women in the military, but they don't put us in the front lines. They don't know if we can fight. I think we can. All the general has to do is walk over to the women and say, 'You see the enemy over there? They say you look fat in those uniforms.'

Elayne Boosler

Cats

A catless writer is almost inconceivable. It's a perverse taste, really, since it would be easier to write with a herd of buffalo in the room than even one cat; they make nests in the notes and bite the end of the pen and walk on the typewriter keys.

Barbara Holland

I found out why cats drink out of the toilet. My mother told me it's because the water is cold in there. And I'm like, how did my mother know that?

Wendy Liebman

Cats regard people as warm-blooded furniture.

Jacquelyn Mitchard

The problem with cats is that they get the exact same look on their face whether they see a moth or an axe-murderer.

Paula Poundstone

A cat is a puzzle for which there is no solution.

Hazel Nicholson

Purring would seem to be an automatic safety valve device for dealing with happiness overflow.

Monica Edwards

After scolding one's cat one looks into its face and is seized by the ugly suspicion that it understood every word – and has filed it for reference.

Charlotte Gray

If there were to be a universal sound depicting peace, I would surely vote for the purr.

Barbara L. Diamond

It is impossible to keep a straight face in the presence of one or more kittens.

Cynthia E. Varnado

Who among us hasn't envied a cat's ability to ignore the cares of daily life and to relax completely?

Karen Brademeyer

A cat improves the garden wall in sunshine, and the hearth in foul weather.

Judith Merkle Riley

Change

A woman may be able to change the world,
but she will never be able to change a man.
Amy Snowden

The only time a woman really succeeds in
changing a man is when he is a baby.
Natalie Wood

Sometimes a single phrase can alter the way we see the world
and forever change the way we see ourselves.
Nora Moran

I've met a few people who had to change their jobs in order to change
their lives, but I've met many more people who merely had to change
their motive to service in order to change their lives.
Peace Pilgrim

Those who expect moments of change to be comfortable
and free of conflict have not learned their history.
Joan Wallach Scott

Continuity gives us roots; change gives us
branches, letting us stretch and grow and
reach new heights.
Pauline R. Kezer

> Life is about how you deal with change.
>
> *Jane Seymour*

That's the risk you take if you change: that people you've been involved with won't like the new you. But other people who do will come along.

Lisa Alther

If you don't like the way the world is, you change it. You have an obligation to change it. You just do it one step at a time.

Marian Wright Edelman

It's the most unhappy people who most fear change.

Mignon McLaughlin

Lasting change is a series of compromises. And compromise is all right, as long your values don't change.

Jane Goodall

Character

The best index to a person's character is (a) how he treats people who can't do him any good, and (b) how he treats people who can't fight back.

Abigail Van Buren

People grow through experience if they meet life honestly and courageously. This is how character is built.

Eleanor Roosevelt

It is not in the still calm of life, or the repose of a pacific station, that great characters are formed... The habits of a vigorous mind are formed in contending with difficulties.

Abigail Adams

God can do nothing while my interest is in my personal character. He will take care of this if I obey His call.

Florence Allshorn

The world may take your reputation from you, but it cannot take your character.

Emma Dunham

Character cannot be developed in ease and quiet. Only through experiences of trial and suffering can the soul be strengthened, vision cleared, ambition inspired and success achieved.

Helen Keller

 Character builds slowly, but it can be torn down within incredible swiftness.

Faith Baldwin

Childhood

Childhood is a short season.

Helen Hayes

A child's world is fresh and new and beautiful, full of wonder and excitement. It is our misfortune that for most of us that clear-eyed vision, which is true instinct for what is beautiful and awe-inspiring, is dimmed and even lost before we reach adulthood.

Rachel Carson

Childhood is the kingdom where nobody dies. Nobody that matters, that is.

Edna St. Vincent Millay

Childhood is the fiery furnace in which we are melted down to essentials and that essential shaped for good.

Katherine Anne Porter

Childhood is the most beautiful of all life's seasons.

Author unknown

Let a man turn to his own childhood – no further – if he will renew his sense of remoteness, and of the mystery of change.

Alice Meynell

The older I grow the more earnestly I feel that the few joys of childhood are the best that life has to give.

Ellen Glasgow

Children

We worry about what a child will become tomorrow, yet we forget that he is someone today.

Stacia Tauscher

Little girls are cute and small only to adults. To one another they are not cute. They are life-sized.

Margaret Atwood

Children's talent to endure stems from their ignorance of alternatives.

Maya Angelou

Women gather together to wear silly hats, eat dainty food, and forget how unresponsive their husbands are. Men gather to talk sports, eat heavy food, and forget how demanding their wives are. Only where children gather is there any real chance of fun.

Mignon McLaughlin

Children seldom misquote – in fact, they usually repeat word for word what you shouldn't have said.

Author unknown

Even when freshly washed and relieved of all obvious confections, children tend to be sticky.

Fran Lebowitz

A parent who has never apologized to his children is a monster. If he's always apologizing, his children are monsters.

Mignon McLaughlin

Sing out loud in the car even, or especially, if it embarrasses your children.

Marilyn Penland

When my kids become wild and unruly, I use a nice, safe playpen. When they're finished, I climb out.

Erma Bombeck

What a child doesn't receive
he can seldom later give.

P.D. James

If your children spend most of their time in other people's houses, you're lucky;
if they all congregate at your house, you're blessed.

Mignon McLaughlin

You will always be your child's favourite toy.

Vicki Lansky

My mom used to say it doesn't matter how many kids you have...
because one kid will take up 100% of your time so more kids can't
possibly take up more than 100% of your time.

Karen Brown

Your children tell you casually years later what it would
have killed you with worry to know at the time.

Mignon McLaughlin

Childraising

There are three reasons
for breast-feeding: the
milk is always at the right
temperature; it comes
in attractive containers;
and the cat can't get it.

Irena Chalmers

Think what a better world
it would be if we all, the
whole world, had cookies
and milk about three o'clock
every afternoon and then
lay down on our blankets for
a nap.

Barbara Jordan

ahhhhhh

**The quickest way for a parent to get a
child's attention is to sit down and look comfortable.**
Lane Olinghouse

If you want your children to keep their feet on the ground –
put some responsibility on their shoulders.
Abigail Van Buren

**Let our children grow tall, and some taller
than others if they have it in them to do so.**
Margaret Thatcher

A child is fed with milk and praise.
Mary Lamb

Love your children with all your hearts; love them enough to discipline them before it is too late... Praise them for important things, even if you have to stretch them a bit. Praise them a lot. They live on it like bread and butter and they need it more than bread and butter.

Lavina Christensen Fugal

We need to teach the next generation of children from Day One that they are responsible for their lives.

Elisabeth Kübler-Ross

There's no road map on how to raise a family: it's always an enormous negotiation.

Meryl Streep

Although there are many trial marriages...there is no such thing as a trial child.

Gail Sheehy

Choice

One's philosophy is not best expressed in words; it is expressed in the choices one makes. In the long run, we shape our lives and we shape ourselves. The process never ends until we die. And, the choices we make are ultimately our own responsibility.

Eleanor Roosevelt

Instead of looking at life as a narrowing funnel, we can see it ever widening to choose the things we want to do, to take the wisdom we've learned and create something.

Liz Carpenter

We are responsible for the quality of our vision, we have a say in the shaping of our sensibility. In the many thousand daily choices we make, we create ourselves and the voice with which we speak and work.

Carolyn Forche

Always go with the choice that scares you the most, because that's the one that is going to require the most from you.

Caroline Myss

I discovered I always have choices and sometimes it's only a choice of attitude.

Judith M. Knowlton

No life is so hard that you can't make it easier by the way you take it.

Ellen Glasgow

It's so hard when I have to, And so easy when I want to.

Sondra Anice Barnes

As simple as it sounds, we all must try to be the best person we can: by making the best choices, by making the most of the talents we've been given.

Mary Lou Retton

Clothes

I don't know who invented the high heel, but all men owe him a lot.

Marilyn Monroe

On the subject of dress almost no one, for one or another reason, feels truly indifferent: if their own clothes do not concern them, somebody else's do.

Elizabeth Bowen

Dress shabbily, they notice the dress. Dress impeccably, they notice the woman.

Gabrielle "Coco" Chanel

The dress must not hang on the body but follow its lines. It must accompany its wearer and when a woman smiles the dress must smile with her.

Madeleine Vionnet

Ninety percent of a woman's wardrobe is never worn. Ninety percent of a woman's wardrobe represents fantasies and despair.

Elizabeth Buchan

Dress is at all times a frivolous distinction, and excessive solicitude about it often destroys its own aim.

Jane Austen

There is something lacking in a professional woman who can't or won't dress well: it's not just about aesthetics, it's about discipline, self-respect, confidence, and, ultimately a capacity for enjoyment

Jo Elvin, Daily Telegraph, 17 April 2008

Clothes can suggest, persuade, connote, insinuate, or indeed lie, and apply subtle pressure while their wearer is speaking frankly and straightforwardly of other matters.

Anne Hollander

British culture does not allow female (politicians) the right to dress stylishly. It is viewed as frivolous and an indication of priorities not being what they should. Elsewhere in the world the fact that a women looks glamorous has no bearing on the calibre of her mind – it is something to be celebrated.

Kim Herzov, Daily Telegraph, 17 April 2008

It is almost as stupid to let your clothes betray that you know you are ugly as to have them proclaim that you think you are beautiful.

Edith Wharton

> There is much to support the view that it is clothes that wear us and not we them; we may make them take the mould of arm or breast, but they would mould our hearts, our brains, our tongues to their liking.
>
> *Virginia Woolf*

Adornment is never anything except a reflection of the heart.

Gabrielle "Coco" Chanel

Fashion can be bought. Style one must possess.

Edna Woolman Chase

Expensive clothes are a waste of money.

Meryl Streep

On the whole, I think women wear too much and are too fussy. You can't see the person for all the clutter.

Julie Andrews

Communication

The most exhausting thing in life, I have discovered, is being insincere. That is why so much social life is exhausting; one is wearing a mask.

Anne Morrow Lindbergh

Letters are venerable; and the telephone valiant, for the journey is a lonely one, and if bound together by notes and telephones we went in company, perhaps – who knows? – we might talk by the way.

Virginia Woolf

Silence is often misinterpreted – but it is never quoted.

Author unknown

The real art of conversation is not only to say the right thing
in the right place but to leave unsaid the wrong thing
at the tempting moment.

Dorothy Nevill

Language exerts hidden power, like the moon on the tides.

Rita Mae Brown

Politeness is the art of selecting among one's real thoughts.

Madame de Staël

Lord – Fill my mouth with worthwhile stuff,
and nudge me when I've said enough!

Anon

A good message will always find a messenger.

Amelia E. Barr

If I'd kept my mouth shut I wouldn't be here!

Sign under a stuffed fish

Confidence

I think we all have inner confidence buried in us – it's just that we sometimes have to dig deep to find it.

Sophie Raworth

You've got to take the initiative and play your game... confidence makes the difference.

Chris Evert

Regardless of how you feel inside, always try to look like a winner. Even if you are behind, a sustained look of control and confidence can give you a mental edge that results in victory.

Diane Arbus

If you can react the same way to winning and losing – that is a big accomplishment. That quality is important because it stays with you the rest of your life.

Chris Evert

It took me a long time not to judge myself through someone else's eyes.

Sally Field

Real confidence comes from knowing and accepting yourself – your strengths and your limitations – in contrast to depending on affirmation from others.

Judith M. Bardwick

I am not a has-been. I am a will-be.

Lauren Bacall

The way you overcome shyness is to become so wrapped up in something that you forget to be afraid.

Lady Bird Johnson

There is safety in reserve, but no attraction. One cannot love a reserved person.
Jane Austen

I like to help women help themselves, as that is, in my opinion, the best way to settle the woman question. Whatever we can do and do well we have a right to, and I don't think anyone will deny us.
Louisa May Alcott

There's nothing enlightened about shrinking so that other people won't feel insecure around you.
Marianne Williamson

Courage

One isn't necessarily born with courage, but one is born with potential. Without courage, we cannot practice any other virtue with consistency. We can't be kind, true, merciful, generous or honest.
Maya Angelou

Courage doesn't always roar. Sometimes courage is the little voice at the end of the day that says I'll try again tomorrow.
Mary Anne Radmacher

Courage is reclaiming your life after a devastating event robs you of your confidence and self-esteem. It is facing tomorrow with a firm resolve to reach deep within yourself to find another strength, another talent... It is taking yourself to another level of your own existence where you are once again whole, productive, special...
Catherine Britton

Bravery is picking yourself up and getting on with it... bravery isn't pretending that the inconvenient truth never happened.

India Knight

Underneath courage shouts fear, but of a hoarse voice.

Irisa Hail

Like gaining confidence, finding one's courage is gradual rather than all at once.

Barbara Barksdale Clowse

Courage is as often the outcome of despair as of hope; in the one case we have nothing to lose, in the other everything to gain.

Diane de Poitiers

<u>Creativity</u>

Creativity is like a great receptive womb.

Lynn V. Andrews

Creative minds always have been known to survive any kind of bad training.

Anna Freud

Real creativity begins with the drive to work on and on and on.

Margueritte Harmon Bro

Creativity can be described as letting go of certainties.

Gail Sheehy

The richest source of creation is feeling, followed by a vision of its meaning.

Anais Nin

Self-forgetfulness in creativity can lead to self-transcendence.

Sylvia Ashton-Warner

Creativity comes by breaking the rules, by saying you're in love with the anarchist.

Anita Roddick

D

Dating

I will **not** go out with a man who wears more jewelry than me, and I'll **never, ever** go to bed with a guy who calls me **Babe**. Other than that, however, I'm real flexible.

Linda Sunshine

> People shop for a bathing suit with more care than they do a husband or wife. The rules are the same. Look for something you'll feel comfortable wearing. Allow for room to grow.
>
> *Erma Bombeck*

I've never been married, but I tell people I'm divorced
so they won't think something's wrong with me.
Elayne Boosler

Ideally, couples need three lives; one for him,
one for her, and one for them together.
Jacqueline Bisset

I've figured out why first dates don't work any better than they do. It's because they take place in restaurants. Women are weird and confused and unhappy about food, and men are weird and confused and unhappy about money, yet off they go, the minute they meet, to where you use money to buy food.
Lara Adair

Plenty of guys are good at sex,
but conversation, now there's an art.
Linda Barnes

My boyfriend and I broke up.
He wanted to get married, and I didn't want him to.
Rita Rudner

Platonic friendship: The interval between the introduction and the first kiss.

Sophie Irene Loeb

Death

Death is the opening of a more subtle life. In the flower, it sets free the perfume; in the chrysalis, the butterfly; in man, the soul.

Juliette Adam

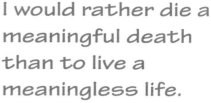

I would rather die a meaningful death than to live a meaningless life.

Corazon Aquino

Death is a tangible reminder that life is too short to not do what you love.

Tammy Cravit

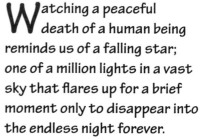

Watching a peaceful death of a human being reminds us of a falling star; one of a million lights in a vast sky that flares up for a brief moment only to disappear into the endless night forever.

Elisabeth Kübler-Ross

There's something about death that is comforting. The thought that you could die tomorrow frees you to appreciate your life now.

Angelina Jolie

I postpone death by living, by suffering, by error, by risking, by giving, by losing.

Anais Nin

We understand death for the first time when he puts his hand upon one whom we love.

Madame de Staël

Decision

No trumpets sound when the important decisions of our life are made.
Destiny is made known silently.
Agnes DeMille

To gain that which is worth having, it may be necessary to lose everything else.
Burnadette Devlin

If you've made up your mind you can do something,
you're absolutely right. If you've made up your mind you can't
do something, you're absolutely right.
Author unknown

Once I decide to do something, I do it. I'm fearless.
Ann M. Fudge

The most difficult thing is the decision to act, the rest is merely tenacity.
The fears are paper tigers. You can do anything you decide to do.
Amelia Earhart

A peacefulness follows any decision – even the wrong one.
Rita Mae Brown

Somewhere along the line of development we discover what we really
are, and then we make our real decision for which we are responsible.
Make that decision primarily for yourself because you can never really
live anyone else's life, not even your own child's.
Eleanor Roosevelt

The thing that's important to know is that you never know.
You're always sort of feeling your way.
Diane Arbus

Despair

There is no despair so absolute as that which comes with the first moments of our first great sorrow, when we have not yet known what it is to have suffered and be healed, to have despaired and have recovered hope.

George Eliot

Think of all the beauty still left around you and be happy.

Anne Frank

Where Christ brings His cross He brings His presence; and where He is none are desolate, and there is no room for despair.

Elizabeth Barrett Browning

Wonder and despair are two sides of a spinning coin. When you open yourself to one, you open yourself to the other. You discover a capacity for joy that wasn't in you before. Wonder is the promise of restoration: as deeply as you dive, so may you rise.

Christina Baldwin

To eat bread without hope is still slowly to starve to death.

Pearl S. Buck

Action is the antidote to despair.

Joan Baez

The fact that God has prohibited despair gives misfortune the right to hope all things, and leaves hope free to dare all things.

Madame Anne Sophie Swetchine

Diet

I feel about airplanes the way I feel about diets. It seems to me that they are wonderful things for other people to go on.

Jean Kerr

There comes a point when the diet stops being a diet and becomes a way of life; no great hardship, believe me, and I write as the greediest person I know.

India Knight

Dieting is wishful shrinking.

Author unknown

Self-love is the only weight loss aid that really works in the long run.

Jenny Craig

I was a vegetarian until I started leaning towards the sunlight.

Rita Rudner

God loves us whether we're 20 stone or whether we're 10 stone. However, I think we do need to respect the bodies that God has given us.

Rosemary Conley

A diet is the penalty we pay for exceeding the feed limit.

Author unknown

Most of us overeat because we're sad, anxious, bored, depressed, or happy, joyous, celebratory (all seven, in my case).

India Knight

I am the one who got myself fat, who did all the eating. So I had to take full responsibility for it.

Kirstie Alley

If I don't eat junk, I don't gain weight.

Paula Christensen

Don't dig your grave with your own knife and fork.

English proverb

We are indeed much more than what we eat, but what we eat can nevertheless help us to be much more than what we are.

Adelle Davis

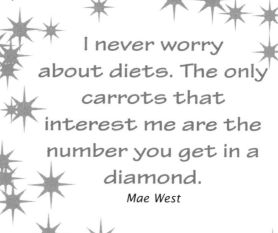

I never worry about diets. The only carrots that interest me are the number you get in a diamond.

Mae West

Difference

As the traveller who has once been from home is wiser than he who has never left his own doorstep, so a knowledge of one other culture should sharpen our ability to scrutinize more steadily, to appreciate more lovingly, our own.

Margaret Mead

We should acknowledge differences; we should greet differences, until difference makes no difference anymore.

Dr Adela A. Allen

The greatest discoveries have come from people who have looked at a standard situation and seen it differently.

Ira Erwin

We must not, in trying to think about how we can make a big difference, ignore the small daily differences we can make which, over time, add up to big differences that we often cannot foresee.

Marian Wright Edelman

In order to be irreplaceable one must always be different.

Gabrielle "Coco" Chanel

Any woman who has a career and a family automatically develops something in the way of two personalities, like two sides of a dollar bill, each different in design... Her problem is to keep one from draining the life from the other.

Ivy Baker Priest

Difficulty

Expect trouble as an inevitable part of life, and when it comes, hold your head high, look it squarely in the eye and say, 'I will be bigger than you. You cannot defeat me.'

Anne Landers

There are some things you learn best in calm, and some in storm.

Willa Sibert Cather

There are two ways of meeting difficulties. You alter the difficulties or you alter yourself to meet them.

Phyllis Bottome

Difficult times always create opportunities for you to experience more love in your life.

Barbara De Angelis

If we can view our trials from the perspective of the end result, we will find them easier to bear. Indeed, we can even experience a sort of inner peace as we keep going.

Mary Pytches

It is a queer thing, but imaginary troubles are harder to bear than actual ones.

Dorothy Dix

Every man deems that he has precisely the trials and temptations which are the hardest of all others for him to bear; but they are so, simply because they are the very ones he most needs.

Lydia M. Child

Discipline

Even though the ship may go down,
the journey goes on.

Margaret Mead

Working hard overcomes a whole lot of other obstacles. You can have unbelievable intelligence, you can have connections, and you can have opportunities fall out of the sky. But in the end, hard work is the true, enduring characteristic of successful people.

Rear Admiral Marsha Evans

Champions know there are no shortcuts to the top. They climb the mountain one step at a time. They have no use for helicopters!

Judi Adler

Lack of discipline leads to frustration and self-loathing.

Marie Chapian

There is no allurement or enticement, actual or imaginary, which a well-disciplined mind may not surmount. The wish to resist more than half accomplishes the object.

Charlotte Dacre

There is no chance, no destiny, no fate that can circumvent or hinder or control the firm resolve of a determined soul.

Ella Wheeler Wilcox

Some people regard discipline as a chore. For me, it is a kind of order that sets me free to fly.

Julie Andrews

Discontentment

I personally think we developed language because of our deep inner need to complain.

Jane Wagner

The way, I think, anything has ever really changed on this planet is through large groups of very ordinary people saying something finally.

Emma Thompson

In trying to get our own way, we should remember that kisses are sweeter than whine.

Source unknown

The poor wish to be rich; the rich wish to be happy. The single wish to be married, and the married wish to be dead.

Ann Landers

Complacency is a far more dangerous attitude than outrage.

Naomi Littlebear Morena

Who is not satisfied with himself will grow; who is not sure of his own correctness will learn many things.

Chinese proverb

> I can't say that the college-bred woman is the most contented woman. The broader her mind the more she understands the unequal conditions between men and women, the more she chafes under a government that tolerates it.
>
> *Susan B. Anthony*

Discouragement

Don't be discouraged by being average at some point in your life.
General Claudia Kennedy

One of the things I learned the hard way was that it doesn't pay to get discouraged. Keeping busy and making optimism a way of life can restore your faith in yourself.

Lucille Ball

The marvellous richness of human experience would lose something of rewarding joy if there were no limitations to overcome. The hilltop hour would not be half so wonderful if there were no dark valleys to traverse.

Helen Keller

It's a terrible thing to go through life thinking that you have a rock on your side when you haven't.

Maria Callas

The most difficult disappointment is when people let you down, that is hard to get over. You must accept it as a lesson learnt.

Esther Rantzen

For a long time it seemed to me that real life was about to begin, but there was always some obstacle in the way. Something had to be got through first, some unfinished business; time still to be served, a debt to be paid. Then life would begin. At last it dawned on me that these obstacles were my life.

Bette Howland

Dogs

Dogs are the most amazing creatures; they give unconditional love. For me they are the role model for being alive.

Gilda Radner

When you feel really lousy, puppy therapy is indicated.

Sara Paretsky

Dogs act exactly the way we would act if we had no shame.

Cynthia Heimel

I wonder if other dogs think poodles are members of some weird religious cult.

Rita Rudner

From the dog's point of view, his master is an elongated and abnormally cunning dog.

Mabel Louise Robinson

A puppy is but a dog, plus high spirits, and minus common sense.

Agnes Repplier

There is no such thing as a difficult dog, only an inexperienced owner.

Barbara Woodhouse

Don't accept your dog's admiration as conclusive evidence that you are wonderful.

Anne Landers

you know - that was a good idea of yours - this is actually rather fun!

If you are a dog and your owner suggests that you wear a sweater, suggest that he wear a tail.

Fran Lebowitz

Did you ever walk into a room and forget why you walked in? I think that's how dogs spend their lives.

Sue Murphy

It's funny how dogs and cats know the inside of folks better than other folks do, isn't it?

Eleanor Porter

Women are like dogs really. They love like dogs, a little insistently. And they like to fetch and carry and come back wistfully after hard words, and learn rather easily to carry a basket.

Mary Roberts Rinehart

Dreams

Dreaming, after all, is a form of planning.
Gloria Steinem

Within your heart, keep one still, secret spot where dreams may go.
Louise Driscoll

I didn't get where I am thinking about it or dreaming it. I got here by doing it.
Estée Lauder

Dreams are illustrations... from the book your soul is writing about you.
Marsha Norman

I believe that everyone is the keeper of a dream –
and by tuning into one another's secret hopes, we can become better friends,
better partners, better parents and better lovers.
Oprah Winfrey

It takes a lot of courage to show your dream to someone else.
Erma Bombeck

Dreams are nature's answering service – don't forget to pick up your messages once in a while.
Sarah Crestinn

To achieve the impossible dream, try going to sleep.
Joan Klempner

E

Education

The highest result of education is tolerance.

Helen Keller

If you think education is expensive, try ignorance.

Emma Goldman

A stale mind is the devil's breadbox.

Mary Bly

It is as impossible to withhold education from the receptive mind, as it is impossible to force it upon the unreasoning.

Agnes Repplier

Educate a woman and you educate a family.

Jovita Idar

The world of education is like an island where people, cut off from the world, are prepared for life by exclusion from it.

Maria Montessori

To be able to be caught up into the world of thought – that is being educated.

Edith Hamilton

Those who have been required to memorize the world as it is will never create the world as it might be.

Judith Groch

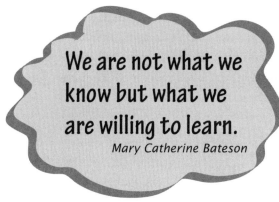

We are not what we know but what we are willing to learn.

Mary Catherine Bateson

Education, fundamentally, is the increase of the percentage of the conscious in relation to the unconscious.

Sylvia Ashton-Warner

Real education should educate us out of self into something far finer; into a selflessness which links us with all humanity.

Nancy Astor

Endurance

Patient endurance attains to all things; who God possesses in nothing is wanting; alone God suffices.

St Teresa of Avila

Endurance is frequently a form of indecision.

Elizabeth Bibesco

True love isn't the kind that endures through long years of absence, but the kind that endures through long years of propinquity.

Helen Rowland

You have to endure what you can't change.

Marie de France

Nothing could be worse than the fear that one had given up too soon, and left one unexpended effort that might have saved the world.

Jane Addams

Whoever said anybody has a right to give up?

Marian Wright Edelman

The very fact that we make such a to-do over golden weddings indicates our amazement at human endurance. The celebration is more in the nature of a reward for stamina.

Ilka Chase

Enthusiasm

It is so much easier to be enthusiastic than to reason!

Eleanor Roosevelt

Enthusiasm is the Spirit of God working with you.

Author unknown

A mediocre idea that generates enthusiasm will go further than a great idea that inspires no one.

Mary Kay Ash

You will do foolish things, but do them with enthusiasm.

Sidonie-Gabrielle Colette

Enthusiasm is a telescope that yanks the misty, distant future into the radiant, tangible present.

Author unknown

Enthusiasm is contagious. Be a carrier.
Susan Rabin

Excellence

The sad truth is that excellence makes people nervous.

Shana Alexander

Do the best you can in every task, no matter how unimportant it may seem at the time. No one learns more about a problem than the person at the bottom.

Sandra Day O'Connor

Striving for excellence motivates you; striving for perfection is demoralizing.

Harriet Braiker

You can't always expect a certain result, but you can expect to do your best.

Anita Hill

The pursuit of excellence is a personal journey into higher realms of existence, a journey that enriches the self and the world through its bounty. It is the crucible that purifies the spirit – the manifestation of life's longing for evolution.

Linda Kreger Silverman

Eagles don't flock.
Ann Winblad

I never practice;
I always play.
Wanda Landowska
(harpsichord master)

The secret of joy in work is contained in one word – excellence. To know how to do something well is to enjoy it.

Pearl S. Buck

If you want to stand out, don't be different, be outstanding.

Meredith West

Expectations

It is great to be a blonde. With low expectations it's very easy to surprise people.
Pamela Anderson

I've always got such high expectations for myself.
I'm aware of them, but I can't relax them.
Mary Decker Stanley (athlete)

What is sad for women of my generation is that they weren't supposed to work if they had families. What were they going to do when the children are grown? Watch the raindrops coming down the windowpane?

Jacqueline Kennedy Onassis

It would be as wise to set up an accomplished lawyer to saw wood as a business as to condemn an educated and sensible woman to spend all her time boiling potatoes and patching old garments. Yet this is the lot of many a one who incessantly stitches and boils and bakes, compelled to thrust back out of sight the aspirations which fill her soul.

Sarah Grimke

A master can tell you what he expects of you. A teacher, though, awakens your own expectations.
Patricia Neal

To free us from the expectations of others, to give us back to ourselves —
there lies the great, singular power of self-respect.
Joan Didion

Experience

If you can learn from hard knocks, you can also learn from soft touches.

Carolyn Kenmore

Good judgment comes from experience, and often experience comes from bad judgment.

Rita Mae Brown

Life is the only real counsellor; wisdom unfiltered through personal experience does not become a part of the moral tissue.

Edith Wharton

Experience is true gold. Experience is what you get when you don't get what you wanted.

Anne Landers

You gain strength, courage and confidence by every experience in which you stop and look fear in the face.

Eleanor Roosevelt

Turn your wounds into wisdom.

Oprah Winfrey

The notion of a university of human experience is a confidence trick and the notion of a universality of female experiences is a clever confidence trick.

Angela Carter

Learning from experience is a faculty almost never practiced.

Barbara Tuchman

If we could sell our experiences for what they cost us, we'd all be millionaires.

Abigail Van Buren

It is strange how often a heart must be broken before the years can make it wise.

Sara Teasdale

There's nothing half so real in life as the things you've done ... inexorably, unalterably done.

Sara Teasdale

F

Failure

Flops are part of life's menu, and I'm never a girl to miss out on any of the courses.

Rosalind Russell

Failure teaches you that you have to be careful. When you look at a glass as being half full, you need to make certain that the variables that fill up that glass are within your reach instead of being controlled by others.

Ann Winblad

Failure? I never encountered it. All I ever met were temporary setbacks.

Dottie Walters

A garden is always a series of losses set against a few triumphs, like life itself.

May Sarton

It is impossible to live without failing at something, unless you live so cautiously that you might as well not have lived at all – in which case, you fail by default.

J.K. Rowling

I am never a failure until I begin blaming others.

Author unknown

The mystery of existence is the connection between our faults and our misfortunes.

Madame de Stael

Faith

Faith is putting all your eggs in God's basket, then counting your blessings before they hatch.

Ramona C. Carroll

Faith walks simply, childlike, between the darkness of human life and the hope of what is to come.

Catherine de Hueck Doherty

Faith is a curious thing. It must be renewed; it has its own spring.

Gladys Taber

Faith is not belief. Belief is passive. Faith is active.

Edith Hamilton

Faith is that quality or power by which the things desired become the things possessed.

Kathryn Kuhlman

Leap, and the net will appear.

Julie Cameron

I would rather walk with God in the dark than go alone in the light.

Mary Gardiner Brainard

Faith and doubt both are needed – not as antagonists, but working side by side to take us around the unknown curve.

Lillian Smith

Weave in faith and God will find the thread.

Author unknown

The prayer that reforms the sinner and heals the sick is an absolute faith that all things are possible to God.

Mary Baker Eddy

Faith is for that which lies on the other side of reason. Faith is what makes life bearable, with all its tragedies and ambiguities and sudden, startling joys.

Madeleine L'Engle

Family

The family... We were a strange little band of characters trudging through life sharing diseases and toothpaste, coveting one another's desserts, hiding shampoo, borrowing money, locking each other out of our rooms, inflicting pain and kissing to heal it in the same instant, loving, laughing, defending and trying to figure out the common thread that bound us all together.

Erma Bombeck

What families have in common the world around is that they are the place where people learn who they are and how to be that way.

Jean Illsley Clarke

Happy or unhappy, families are all mysterious.

Gloria Steinem

Heirlooms we don't have in our family. But stories we've got.

Rose Cherin

I think togetherness is a very important ingredient to family life.

Barbara Bush

To the outside world we all grow old. But not to brothers and sisters. We know each other as we always were. We know each other's hearts. We share private family jokes. We remember family feuds and secrets, family griefs and joys. We live outside the touch of time.

Clara Ortega

Family is just accident... They don't mean to get on your nerves. They don't even mean to be your family, they just are.

Marsha Norman

Family faces are magic mirrors. Looking at people who belong to us, we see the past, present and future. We make discoveries about ourselves.

Gail Lumet Buckley

Nobody, who has not been in the interior of a family, can say what the difficulties of any individual of that family may be.

Jane Austen

Call it a clan, call it a network, call it a tribe, call it a family. Whatever you call it, whoever you are, you need one.

Jane Howard

Unkindness is death to the home. One unkind, unsocial, critical, eternally dissatisfied member can destroy any family.

Kathleen Norris

In some families, please is described as the magic word. In our house, however, it was sorry.

Margaret Laurence

The great advantage of living in a large family is that early lesson of life's essential unfairness.

Nancy Mitford

Fashion

Fashion, the constant and needless change of things, is fast becoming one of the greater ills of all time.

Elizabeth Hawes

My mother insisted that I had to try things on to make sure they were becoming. Becoming what, I always asked.

Edith Konecky

So soon as a fashion is universal, it is out of date.

Marie von Ebner-Eschenbach

No fashion has ever been created expressly for the lean purse or for the fat woman: the dressmaker's ideal is the thin millionaires.

Katherine Fullerton Gerould

To call fashion wearable is the kiss of death. No new fashion worth its salt is ever wearable.

Eugenia Sheppard

Money has nothing to do with style at all, but naturally it helps in every situation.

Diana Vreeland

It is not chic to be too chic.

Elsie de Wolfe

I base most of my fashion taste on what doesn't itch.

Gilda Radner

Does fashion matter? Always – though not quite as much after death.

Joan Rivers

Fashion, as we knew it, is over; people wear now exactly what they feel like wearing.

Mary Quant

Fashion seems to exist for an abstract person who is not you or me.

Elizabeth Bowen

Fashion can be bought... style one must possess.

Edna Woolman Chase

Fear

Fear is faith that it won't work out.

Sister Mary Tricky

I'm not afraid of storms, for I'm learning to sail my ship.

Louisa May Alcott

We don't have to wait for fear to vanish altogether because that moment will never come; all we need is a moment of daring that can change a whole lifetime of waiting.

Diane Conway

Anything I've ever done that ultimately was worthwhile... initially scared me to death.

Dorothy Bender

Do what you are afraid to do.

Mary Emerson

Fear is a question: What are you afraid of, and why? Just as the seed of health is in illness, because illness contains information, our fears are a treasure house of self-knowledge if we explore them.

Marilyn Ferguson

Our deepest fear is not that we are inadequate. Our deepest fear is that we are powerful beyond measure.

Marianne Williamson

Only when we are no longer afraid do we begin to live.

Dorothy Thompson

Feeling

Better to be without logic than without feeling.

Charlotte Bronte

Our feelings are our most genuine paths to knowledge.

Audre Lorde

You cannot know what you do not feel.

Marya Mannes

Human relations are built on feeling, not on reason or knowledge. And feeling is not an exact science; like all spiritual qualities, it has the vagueness of greatness about it.

Amelia E. Barr

The wide discrepancy between reason and feeling may be unreal; it is not improbable that intellect is a high form of feeling – a specialized, intensive feeling about intuitions.

Susanna K. Langer

Our society allows people to be absolutely neurotic and totally out of touch with their feelings and everyone else's feelings, and yet be very respectful.

Ntozake Shange

It was one of those dangerous moments when speech is at once sincere and deceptive – when feeling, rising high above its average depth, leaves flood-marks which are never reached again.

George Eliot

Why is it that people who cannot show feeling presume that that is a strength and not a weakness?

May Sarton

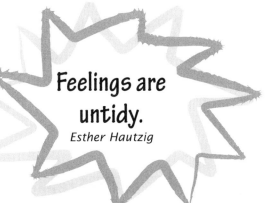

Feelings are untidy.
Esther Hautzig

Atrophy of feeling creates criminals.

Anais Nin

Food

Make food a very incidental part of your life by filling your life so full of meaningful things that you'll hardly have time to think about food.

Peace Pilgrim

Cooking is just as creative and imaginative an activity as drawing, or wood carving, or music. And cooking draws upon your every talent – science, mathematics, energy, history, experience – and the more experience you have, the less likely are your experiments to end in drivel and disaster. The more you know, the more you can create.

Julia Child

Bread and butter, devoid of charm in the drawing-room, is ambrosia eating under a tree.

Elizabeth Russell

Fish, to taste right, must swim three times – in water, in butter, and in wine.

Polish Proverb

Shipping is a terrible thing to do to vegetables. They probably get jet-lagged, just like people.

Elizabeth Berry

Food is the most primitive form of comfort.

Sheila Graham

Whenever you see food beautifully arranged on a plate, you know someone's fingers have been all over it.

Source Unknown

Forgiveness

Once a woman has forgiven her man, she must not reheat his sins for breakfast.

Marlene Dietrich

Forgive all who have offended you, not for them, but for yourself.

Harriet Nelson

Forgiveness is no longer an option but a necessity for healing.

Caroline Myss

Standing as I do, in view of God and eternity, I realize that patriotism is not enough. I must have no hatred or bitterness towards anyone.

Edith Cavell
(spoken before her execution by the Germans on charges of spying, 1915)

You will turn over many a futile new leaf till you learn we must all write on scratched-out pages.

Mignon McLaughlin

The practice of forgiveness is our most important contribution to the healing of the world.

Marianne Williamson

The heart of a mother is a deep abyss at the bottom of which you will always find forgiveness.

Honore de Balzac

Nothing brings families together faster than forgiveness. That should make it Step No. 1, but most of us find forgiving hard. We associate it with weakness and losing when, actually, the reverse is true. When you forgive, you gain strength and come out a winner. You break free of control by the other person's actions.

Joyce Brothers

The forgiving heart is capable of anything

Caroline Myss

It is very easy to forgive others their mistakes. It takes more grit and gumption to forgive them for having witnessed your own.

Jessamyn West

Freedom

To be one's own master is to
be the slave of self.

Natalie Clifford Barney

*I prefer liberty to chains of
diamonds.*

Lady Mary Wortley Montagu

**All the world's
a cage.**

Heanne Philips

**Freedom is always and
exclusively freedom for
the one who thinks
differently.**

Rosa Luxemburg

Freedom is fragile and must be
protected. To sacrifice it, even as
a temporary measure, is to betray it.

Germaine Greer

A free race cannot be
born of slave mothers.

Margaret Sanger

None who have always been
free can understand the
terrible fascinating power
of the hope of freedom to those
who are not free.

Pearl S. Buck

Freedom means
choosing your burden.

Hephzibah Menuhin

Alone I am
free – I am
THE CAT.

Leila Usher

Friendship

A friend is one who knows all about you and likes you anyway.

Christi Mary Warner

You really have to work hard at any relationship and too many friends don't realise that. I think some people take friendship for granted.

Lucy Davis

What a delight it is to make friends with someone you have despised!

Sidonie-Gabrielle Colette

Friendship is not possible between two women, one of whom is very well dressed.

Laurie Colwin

Everyone is your best friend when you are successful. Make sure that the people that you surround yourself with are also the people that you are not afraid of failing with.

Paula Abdul

No person is your friend who demands your silence, or denies your right to grow.

Alice Walker

True friends are those who really know you but love you anyway.

Edna Buchanan

Each friend represents a world in us, a world possibly not born until they arrive, and it's only by this meeting that a new world is born.

Anais Nin

Friendship has no civil, and few emotional, rights in our society.

Christina Baldwin

I suppose there is one friend in the life of each of us who seems not a separate person, however dear and beloved, but an expansion, an interpretation, of one's self, the very meaning of one's soul.

Edith Wharton

[Friendships] are easy to get out of compared to love affairs, but they are not easy to get out of compared to, say, jail.

Fran Lebowitz

Female friendships that work are relationships in which women help each other to belong to themselves.

Louise Bernikow

Business, you know, may bring money, but friendship hardly ever does.

Jane Austen

There are people whom one loves immediately and forever. Even to know they are alive in the world with one is quite enough.

Nancy Spain

Prosperity provideth, but adversity proveth friends.

Queen Elizabeth I

A friend is one who withholds judgment no matter how long you have her unanswered letter.

Sophie Irene Loeb

True friendship is never tranquil.

Marie de Rabutin-Chantal

Future

Through the law of cause and effect we choose our destiny. Moreover, we are our own prophets for we constantly project our future state by the seeds we plant in the present.

Cheryl Canfield

The future belongs to those who believe in the beauty of their dreams.

Eleanor Roosevelt

This is the precept by which I have lived: Prepare for the worst; expect the best; and take what comes.

Hannah Arendt

The history of all times, and of today especially, teaches that... women will be forgotten if they forget to think about themselves.

Louise Otto

I never have plans for the future as you never know how things will turn out.

Nigella Lawson

Our faith in the present dies out long before our faith in the future.

Ruth Benedict

G

Gardening

Gardening is not a rational act.
Margaret Atwood

Gardening has compensations out of all proportion to its goals. It is creation in the pure sense.
Phyllis McGinley

The trouble with gardening… is that it does not remain an avocation. It becomes an obsession.
Phyllis McGinley

The greatest gift of the garden is the restoration of the five senses.
Hanna Rion

Gardening is a madness, a folly that does not go away with age. Quite the contrary.
May Sarton

We have descended into the garden and caught three hundred slugs. How I love the mixture of the beautiful and the squalid in gardening. It makes it so lifelike.
Evelyn Underhill

A garden isn't meant to be useful. It's for joy.
Rumer Godden

Gardens are the result of a collaboration between art and nature.
Penelope Hobhouse

There's little risk in becoming overly proud of one's garden because by its very nature it is humbling. It has a way of keeping you on your knees.
Joann R. Barwick

Each garden has its own surprise.
Susan Allen Toth

There is a kind of immortality in every garden.
Gladys Taber

A garden has a curious innocent way of consuming cash while all the time you are under the illusion that you are spending nothing.
Esther Meynell

Generosity

Ask your child what he wants for dinner only if he's buying.
Fran Lebowitz

Trees outstrip most people in the extent and depth of their work for the public good.
Sara Ebenreck

In helping others, we shall help ourselves, for whatever good we give out completes the circle and comes back to us.

Flora Edwards

I've learned that you shouldn't go through life with a catcher's mitt on both hands; you need to be able to throw something back.

Maya Angelou

Every year I live I am more convinced that the waste of life lies in the love we have not given, the powers we have not used, the selfish prudence that will risk nothing, and which shirking pain, misses happiness as well. No one ever yet was the poorer in the long run for having once in a lifetime let out all the length of all the reins.

Mary Cholmondeley

Go the extra mile. It's never crowded.

Author unknown

Giving frees us from the familiar territory of our own needs by opening our mind to the unexplained worlds occupied by the needs of others.

Barbara Bush

The Lord loveth a cheerful giver. He also accepteth from a grouch.

Catherine Hall

Love never reasons but profusely gives; gives, like a thoughtless prodigal, its all, and trembles lest it has done too little.

Hannah Moore

> *G*iving presents is a talent; to know what a person wants, to know when and how to get it, to give it lovingly and well. Unless a character possesses this talent there is no moment more annihilating to ease than that in which a present is received and given.
>
> *Pamela Glenconner*

Giving

I have come to believe that giving and receiving are really the same. Giving and receiving – not giving and taking.

Joyce Grenfell

To give without any reward, or any notice, has a special quality of its own.

Anne Morrow Lindbergh

Lots of people think they're charitable if they give away their old clothes and things they don't want.

Myrtle Reed

It isn't the size of the gift that matters, but the size of the heart that gives it.

Quoted in The Angels' Little Instruction Book *by Eileen Elias Freeman, Zondervan, 1994.*

Each day comes bearing its own gifts. Untie the ribbons.

Ruth Ann Schabacker

God's gifts put man's best dreams to shame.

Elizabeth Barrett Browning

The best thing to give to your enemy is forgiveness; to an opponent tolerance; to a friend your heart; to your child a good example; to a father deference; to your mother, conduct that will make her proud of you; to yourself respect; and to all men charity.

Frances Balfour

Giving is a joy if we do it in the right spirit.
It all depends on whether we think of it as
'What can I spare?' or as 'What can I share?'

Esther Baldwin York

God

When we can't piece together the puzzle of our own lives, remember the best view of a puzzle is from above. Let Him help put you together.

Amethyst Snow-Rivers

How tired God must be of guilt and loneliness, for that is all we ever bring to Him.

Mignon McLaughlin

Every evening I turn my worries over to God. He's going to be up all night anyway.

Mary C. Crowley

The experience of God, or in any case the possibility of experiencing God, is innate.

Alice Walker

We can only know one thing about God – that he is what we are not. Our wretchedness alone is an image of this. The more we contemplate it, the more we contemplate Him.

Simone Weil

I find it interesting that the meanest life, the poorest existence, is attributed to God's will, but as human beings become more affluent, as their living standard and style begin to ascend the material scale, God descends the scale of responsibility at a commensurate speed.

Maya Angelou

The Character and Nature of God

Malachi 3:3 says: "He will sit as a refiner and purifier of silver."

This verse puzzled some women in a Bible study and they wondered what this statement meant about the character and nature of God.

One of the women offered to find out the process of refining silver and get back to the group at their next Bible study. That week, the woman called a silversmith and made an appointment to watch him at work. She didn't mention anything about the reason for her interest beyond her curiosity about the process of refining silver.

As she watched the silversmith, he held a piece of silver over the fire and let it heat up. He explained that in refining silver, one needed to hold the silver in the middle of the fire where the flames were hottest so as to burn away all the impurities.

The woman thought about God holding us in such a hot spot. Then she thought again about the verse that says: "He sits as a refiner and purifier of silver."

She asked the silversmith if it was true that he had to sit there in front of the fire the whole time the silver was being refined.

The man answered that yes, he not only had to sit there holding the silver, but he had to keep his eyes on the silver the entire time it was in the fire. If the silver was left a moment too long in the flames, it would be destroyed.

The woman was silent for a moment. Then she asked the silversmith, "How do you know when the silver is fully refined?" He smiled at her and answered, "Oh, that's easy – when I see my image in it."

If today you are feeling the heat of the fire, remember that God has His eye on you and will keep watching you until He sees His image in you.

www.heaveninspirations.com/silversmith

Author unknown

People see God every day –
they just don't recognize Him.

Pearl Bailey

I truly and utterly believe.
It is an enormous part of who I am.
Everyone says about me that my
recipes work, well, I know
that God works.
Delia Smith

❝ To God alone be
the glory, for it is
He that does all
things. ❞

*Blessed Marie of the
Incarnation (1599–1672)*

Gossip

I don't care what is written about me as long as it isn't true.

Katharine Hepburn

Great minds discuss ideas, average minds discuss events, small minds discuss people.

Eleanor Roosevelt

Gossip is the opiate of the oppressed.
Erica Jong

Gossip is a sort of smoke that comes from the dirty tobacco-pipes of those who diffuse it; it proves nothing but the bad taste of the smoker.

George Eliot

It's careless talk that deals in polite fiction. It's nasty speculation that's based on not so polite fact. How do we protect ourselves from the venomous sting of such idle gossip? The best way is just to tell the truth and wait for people to start talking about someone else.

Mary Alice Young

Gossip, even when it avoids the sexual, bears about it a faint flavour of the erotic.

Patricia Meyer Spacks

Good gossip approximates art.
Rachel M. Brownstein

The nice thing about egotists is that they don't talk about other people.

Lucille S. Harper

Gossip is just news running ahead of itself in a red satin dress.

Liz Smith

Gratitude

Gratitude helps you to grow and expand. Gratitude brings joy and laughter into your lives and into the lives of all those around you.

Eileen Caddy

One can never pay in gratitude; one can pay 'in kind' somewhere else in life.

Anne Morrow Lindbergh

As each day comes to us refreshed and anew, so does my gratitude renew itself daily. The breaking of the sun over the horizon is my grateful heart dawning upon a blessed world.

Adabella Radici

Feeling grateful or appreciative of someone or something in your life actually attracts more of the things that you appreciate and value into your life.

Christiane Northrup

Silent gratitude isn't much use to anyone.

Gladys Browyn Stern

We often take for granted the very things that most deserve our gratitude.

Cynthia Ozick

Gratitude unlocks the fullness of life. It turns what we have into enough, and more. It turns denial into acceptance, chaos into order, confusion into clarity... It turns problems into gifts, failures into success, the unexpected into perfect timing, and mistakes into important events. Gratitude makes sense of our past, brings peace for today and creates a vision for tomorrow.

Melodie Beattie

Grief

Those who are unhappy have no need for anything in this world but people capable of giving them their attention.

Simone Weil

I learned, when hit by loss, to ask the right question: What next? instead of Why me?... Whenever I am willing to ask What is necessary next? I have moved ahead. Whenever I have taken No for a final answer I have stalled and got stuck.

Julia Cameron

I love my past. I love my present. I'm not ashamed of what I've had, and I'm not sad because I have it no longer.

Sidonie-Gabrielle Colette

Death leaves a heartache no one can heal, love leaves a memory no one can steal.

Inscription on a headstone

It's so curious: one can resist tears and 'behave' very well in the hardest hours of grief. But then someone makes you a friendly sign behind a window, or one notices that a flower that was in bud only yesterday has suddenly blossomed, or a letter slips from a drawer... and everything collapses.

Colette

Invisible tears are the hardest to wipe away.
Just let it out, my friend.

Adabella Radici

Those who don't know how
to weep with their whole
heart don't know how to
laugh either.

Golda Meir

There is a kind of
euphoria of grief, a
degree of madness.

Nigella Lawson

You're not
going to live
your life
unscathed.

Kirstie Alley

Grief can't be shared.
Everyone carries it
alone. His own burden
in his own way.

Anne Morrow Lindbergh

Time engraves our faces
with all the tears we
have not shed.

Natalie Clifford Barney

What soap is for the body,
tears are for the soul.

Jewish proverb

Growth

It is only through disruptions and confusion that we grow, jarred out
of ourselves by the collision of someone else's private world with our
own.

Joyce Carol Oates

Our consciousness rarely registers the beginning of a growth within us any
more than without us: There have been many circulations of the sap before we
detect the smallest sign of the bud.

George Eliot

Advances are made by those with at least a touch of irrational confidence in what they can do.

Joan L. Curcio

All my growth and development led me to believe that if you really do the right thing, and if you play by the rules, and if you've got good enough, solid judgment and common sense, that you're going to be able to do whatever you want to do with your life.

Barbara Jordan

Like a plant that starts up in showers and sunshine and does not know which has best helped it to grow, it is difficult to say whether the hard things or the pleasant things did me the most good.

Lucy Larcom

I hope you will go out and let stories happen to you, and that you will work them, water them with your blood and tears and your laughter till they bloom, till you yourself burst into bloom.

Clarissa Pinkola Estes

Only people who die very young learn all they really need to know in kindergarten.

Wendy Kaminer

What other people, real or imaginary, do and think and feel is an essential guide to our understanding of what we ourselves are and may become.

Ursula K. Le Guin

Life is change: growth is optional.

Karen Kaiser Clark

Authentic Christianity never destroys what is good. It makes it grow, transfigures it, and enriches itself from it.

Claire Huchet Bishop

If we don't change, we don't grow. If we don't grow, we are not really living. Growth demands a temporary surrender of security.

Gail Sheehy

Guilt

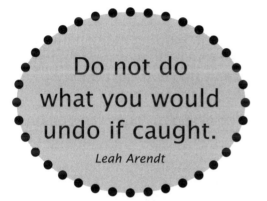

Do not do what you would undo if caught.

Leah Arendt

Mothers, food, love, and career: the four major guilt groups.

Cathy Guisewhite

Guilt is one burden human beings can't bear alone.

Anais Nin

I have no creative use for guilt, yours or my own. Guilt is only another way of avoiding informed action, of buying time out of the pressing need to make clear choices, out of the approaching storm that can feed the earth as well as bend the trees.

Audre Lorde

Show me a woman who doesn't feel guilty and I'll show you a man.

Erica Jong

Guilt is... the next best thing to being there.

Ellen Sue Stern

Guilt: the gift that keeps on giving.

Erma Bombeck

Guilt is the teacher, love is the lesson.

Joan Borysenko

My mother could make anybody feel guilty – she used to get letters of apology from people she didn't even know.

Joan Rivers

No-fault guilt: This is when, instead of trying to figure out who's to blame, everyone pays.

Judith Viorst

She felt that old generic guilt, the kind you feel even when you can't think of what in the world you are supposed to have done.

Meg Wolitzer

For the guilty there is no peace.

Mary Shelley

Guilt is often an excuse for not thinking.

Lillian Hellman

H

Habits

Rigid, the skeleton of habit alone upholds the human frame.

Virginia Woolf

Curious things, habits. People themselves never knew they had them.

Agatha Christie

The power of habit and the charm of novelty are the two adverse forces which explain the follies of mankind.

Maria De Beausacq

Habits, though in their commencement like the filmy line of the spider, trembling at every breeze, may in the end prove as links of tempered steel, binding a deathless being to eternal felicity or woe.

Lydia Huntley Sigourney

Habits of thought persist through the centuries; and while a healthy brain may reject the doctrine it no longer believes, it will continue to feel the same sentiments formerly associated with that doctrine.

Charlotte Perkins Gilman

Small habits well pursued betimes
May reach the dignity of crimes.
Hannah More

Stop the habit of wishful thinking and start the habit of thoughtful wishes.

Mary Martin

In early childhood you may lay the foundation of poverty or riches, industry of idleness, good or evil, by the habits to which you train your children. Teach them right habits then, and their future life is safe.

Lydia Huntley Sigourney

Happiness

Happiness is spiritual, born of Truth and Love. It is unselfish; therefore it cannot exist alone, but requires all mankind to share it.

Mary Baker Eddy

The happiest women, like the happiest nations, have no history.

George Eliot

It is only possible to live happily ever after on a day to day basis.

Margaret Bonnano

Happiness is the ability to recognize it.

Carolyn Wells

A sure way to lose happiness, I found, is to want it at the expense of everything else.

Bette Davis

What is happiness? To be dissolved into something complete and great.

Willa Sibert Cather

Whoever is happy will make others happy, too.

Anne Frank

Happiness must be cultivated. It is like character. It is not a thing to be safely let alone for a moment, or it will run to weeds.

Elizabeth Stuart Phelps

When a small child I thought that success spelled happiness. I was wrong – happiness is like a butterfly which appears and delights us for one brief moment, but soon flits away.

Anna Pavlova

Someday you will find out that there is far more happiness in another's happiness than in your own. It is something I cannot explain, something within that sends a glow of warmth all through you.

Honore de Balzac

Getting what you go after is success; but liking it while you are getting it is happiness.

Bertha Damon

Happiness is a state of consciousness which proceeds from the achievement of one's values.

Ayn Rand

The way to achieve happiness is to have a high standard for yourself and a medium one for everyone else.

Marcelene Cox

Happiness lies in the consciousness we have of it.

George Sand

No one has a right to consume happiness without producing it.

Helen Keller

How little has situation to do with happiness!

Fanny Burney

When one door of happiness closes, another opens; but we look so long at the closed door that we do not see the one which has been opened for us.

Helen Keller

Happiness is not a possession to be prized; it is a quality of thought, a state of mind.

Daphne du Maurier

Happiness is not a station you arrive at, but a manner of travelling.

Margaret Lee Runbeck

Happiness is a tide: it carries you only a little way at a time; but you have covered a vast space before you know that you are moving at all.

Mary Adams

The only people who are truly happy are the people we do not know very well.

Susan Isaacs

Many persons have a wrong idea of what constitutes real happiness. It is not obtained through self-gratification but through fidelity to a worthy purpose.

Helen Keller

The key to happiness and youth is an unencumbered spirit – whether it comes naturally or whether you have to work hard for it.

Emme Woodhull-Bäche

Hate

Hatred is a boomerang which is sure to hit you harder than the one at whom you throw it.

Author unknown

Hate cages all the good things about you.

Madrianne Arvore

There is something to that old saying that hate injures the hater, not the hated.

Peace Pilgrim

You lose a lot of time, hating people.

Marian Anderson

Love lights more fires than hate extinguishes.

Ella Wheeler Wilcox

If we miraculously became the people we hate, how lovable we would find ourselves.

Author unknown

Health

The healthy, the strong individual, is the one who asks for help when he needs it. Whether he has an abscess on his knee or in his soul.

Rona Barrett

I see rejection in my skin, worry in my cancers, bitterness and hate in my aching joints. I failed to take care of my mind, and so my body now goes to hospital.

Astrid Alauda

It's bizarre that the produce manager is more important to my children's health than the paediatrician.

Meryl Streep

An illness of the mind is an illness of the body, and vice versa.

Madrianne Arvore

My fat scares me – it's a ticking time bomb.

Carrie Latet

For fast-acting relief, try slowing down.

Lily Tomlin

Some people think that doctors and nurses can put scrambled eggs back into the shell.

Dorothy Canfield Fisher

I don't eat junk foods and I don't think junk thoughts.

Peace Pilgrim

Everyone who is born holds dual citizenship, in the kingdom of the well and in the kingdom of the sick. Although we all prefer to use only the good passport, sooner or later each of us is obliged, at least for a spell, to identify ourselves as citizens of that other place.

Susan Sontag

Heartache

Where you used to be, there is a hole in the world, which I find myself constantly walking around in the daytime, and falling in at night. I miss you like hell.

Edna St Vincent Millay

Tears may be dried up, but the heart – never.

Marguerite Gardiner

When love is lost, do not bow your head in sadness; instead keep your head up high and gaze into heaven for that is where your broken heart has been sent to heal.

Author unknown

In the arithmetic of love, one plus one equals everything, and two minus one equals nothing.

Mignon McLaughlin

Falling out of love is very enlightening. For a short while you see the world with new eyes.

Iris Murdoch

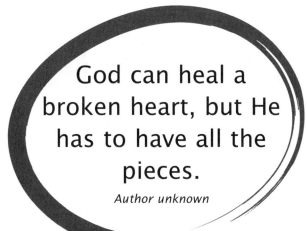

God can heal a broken heart, but He has to have all the pieces.

Author unknown

I don't know why they call it heartbreak. It feels like every other part of my body is broken too.

Missy Altijd

Have you ever been hurt and the place tries to heal a bit, and you just pull the scar off of it over and over again.

Rosa Parks

Heroism

It's true that heroes are inspiring, but mustn't they also do some rescuing if they are to be worthy of their name? Would Wonder Woman matter if she only sent commiserating telegrams to the distressed?

Jeanette Winterson

A hero is simply someone who rises above his own human weaknesses, for an hour, a day, a year, to do something stirring.

Betty Deramus

How important it is for us to recognize and celebrate our heroes and she-roes!

Maya Angelou

We relish news of our heroes, forgetting that we are extraordinary to somebody too.

Helen Hayes

Each woman is far from average in the daily heroics of her life, even though she may never receive a moment's recognition in history.

Women and Work *(Newsage Press)*

A hero is someone we can admire without apology.

Kitty Kelley

Most people aren't appreciated enough, and the bravest things we do in our lives are usually known only to ourselves. No one throws ticker tape on the man who chose to be faithful to his wife, on the lawyer who didn't take the drug money, or the daughter who held her tongue again and again. All this anonymous heroism.

Peggy Noonan

Home

A house that does not have one worn, comfy chair in it is soulless.

May Sarton

Home is a place not only of strong affections, but of entire unreserve; it is life's undress rehearsal, its backroom, its dressing room.

Harriet Beecher Stowe

Home ought to be our clearinghouse, the place from which we go forth lessoned and disciplined, and ready for life.

Kathleen Norris

Home is any four walls that enclose the right person.

Helen Rowland

There is nothing like staying at home for real comfort.

Jane Austen

Home - that blessed word, which opens to the human heart the most perfect glimpse of Heaven, and helps to carry it thither, as on an angel's wings.

Lydia M.Child

Peace - that was the other name for home.

Kathleen Norris

The ideal home: big enough for you to hear the children, but not very well.

Mignon McLaughlin

Honesty

'Honesty' without compassion and understanding is not honesty, but subtle hostility.

Rose N. Franzblau

The most exhausting thing in life is being insincere.

Anne Morrow Lindbergh

A
half truth
is a whole lie.

Yiddish proverb

You never find yourself until you face the truth.

Pearl Bailey

The great advantage about telling the truth is that nobody ever believes it.

Dorothy L. Sayers

The naked truth is always better than the best-dressed lie.

Ann Landers

The woman whose behaviour indicates that she will make a scene if she is told the truth asks to be deceived.

Elizabeth Jenkins

Pain reaches the heart with electrical speed, but truth moves to the heart as slowly as a glacier.

Barbara Kingsolver

Spiritual empowerment is evidenced in our lives by our willingness to tell ourselves the truth, to listen to the truth when it's told to us, and to dispense truth as lovingly as possible, when we feel compelled to talk from the heart.

Christina Baldwin

Hope

Dwell in possibility.
Emily Dickinson

Hope is the denial of reality.

Margaret Wies

The very least you can do in your life is to figure out what you hope for. And the most you can do is live inside that hope.

Barbara Kingsolver

Hope is a very unruly emotion.

Gloria Steinem

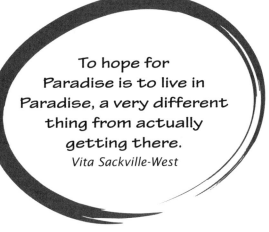

To hope for Paradise is to live in Paradise, a very different thing from actually getting there.
Vita Sackville-West

Hope is slowly extinguished and quickly revived.

Sophia Lee

Hope is the feeling we have that the feeling we have is not permanent.

Mignon McLaughlin

Hope costs nothing.
Sidonie-Gabrielle Colette

Housekeeping

Keeping house is like stringing beads with no knot in the end of the thread.

Author unknown

Housekeeping ain't no joke.

Louisa May Alcott

Invisible, repetitive, exhausting, unproductive, uncreative – these are the adjectives which most perfectly capture the nature of housework.

Angela Davis

No longer will we [women] agree to protect the hearth at the price of extinguishing the fire within ourselves.

Celia Gilbert

The worst thing about work in the house or home is that whatever you do it is destroyed, laid waste or eaten within twenty-four hours.

Lady Hasluck

Housekeeping is like being caught in a revolving door.

Marcelene Cox

I think housework is far more tiring and frightening than hunting is, no comparison, and yet after hunting we had eggs for tea and were made to rest for hours, but after housework people expect one to go on just as if nothing special had happened.

Nancy Mitford

Cleaning your house while your kids are still growing is like shovelling the walk before it stops snowing.

Phyllis Diller

At the worst, a house unkept cannot be so distressing as a life unlived.

Rose Macaulay

I am thankful for a lawn that needs mowing, windows that need cleaning and gutters that need fixing because it means I have a home... I am thankful for the piles of laundry and ironing because it means my loved ones are nearby.

Nancie J. Carmody

A sparkling house is a fine thing if the children aren't robbed of their luster in keeping it that way.

Marcelene Cox

A man would prefer to come home to an unmade bed and a happy woman, than to a neatly made bed and an angry woman.

Marlene Dietrich

The house a woman creates is a Utopia. She can't help it — can't help trying to interest her nearest and dearest not in happiness itself but in the search for it.

Marguerite Duras

Humour

Humour distorts nothing, and only false gods are laughed off their earthly pedestals.

Agnes Repplier

Warning: Humour may be hazardous to your illness.

Ellie Katz

There's a hell of a distance between wisecracking and wit. Wit has truth in it; while wisecracking is simply calisthenics with words.

Dorothy Parker

The truth I do not dare to know
I muffle with a jest.

Emily Dickinson

Total absence of humour renders life impossible.

Sidonie-Gabrielle Colette

Humour is the first of the gifts to perish in a foreign tongue.

Virginia Woolf

Humour is a rubber sword – it allows you to make a point without drawing blood.

Mary Hirsch

Humour and satire are more effective techniques for expressing social statements than direct comment.

Kristin Hunter

A difference of taste in jokes is a great strain on the affections.

George Eliot

Humour tells you where the trouble is.

Louise Bernikow

Ideas

If you have an idea, someone else has it too.

Julie Wainwright

It's not a bad idea to get in the habit of writing down one's thoughts. It saves one having to bother anyone with them.

Isabel Colegate

Ideas that escape are fast and slippery and not likely to be hunted down.

Carrie Latet

Let your working ideas go for a picnic – sometimes the fresh air and ant bites are just what they need. Many great ideas were bitten a little at the beginning.

Carrie Latet

An apathetic or hostile attitude is the enemy of creative thought. Ideas, like people, flourish when they are welcomed and embraced.

Barbara J. Winter

A mediocre idea that generates enthusiasm will go farther than a great idea that inspires no one.

Mary Kay Ash

Night time is really the best time to work. All the ideas are there to be yours because everyone else is asleep.

Catherine O'Hara

Ideas move fast when their time comes.

Carolyn Heilbrun

Who left their ideas in here again?!

A half-baked idea is okay as long as it's in the oven.

Author unknown

Identity

I am constantly writing autobiography, but I have to turn it into fiction in order to give it credibility.

Katherine Paterson

Let the world know you as you are, not as you think you should be, because sooner or later, if you are posing, you will forget the pose, and then where are you?

Fanny Brice

It is much more important to be yourself than anyone else.

Virginia Woolf

These are very confusing times. For the first time in history a woman is expected to combine intelligence with a sharp hairdo, a raised consciousness with high heels.

Lynda Barry

The woman who feels that she is nothing unless she is constantly giving, who is in constant need of reassurance, or who falls into the martyr role... creates misery for others as well as herself.

Grace Baruch, Rosalind Barnett & Caryl Rivers

How many cares one loses when one decides not to be something but to be someone.

Gabrielle "Coco" Chanel

Take back the beauty and wit you bestow upon me; leave me my own mediocrity of agreeableness and genius, but leave me also my sincerity, my constancy, and my plain dealing; 'tis all I have to recommend me to the esteem either of others or myself.

Mary Wortley Montagu

Imagination

Imagination makes cowards of us all.

Ethel Watts Mumford

The imagination needs moodling – long, inefficient, happy idling, dawdling and puttering.

Brenda Ueland

The Possible's slow fuse is lit / By the Imagination.

Emily Dickinson

When you stop having dreams and ideals – well, you might as well stop altogether.

Marian Anderson

The curse of human nature is imagination. When a long anticipated moment comes, we always find it pitched a note too low.

Gertrude Atherton

Imagination is the highest kite that can fly.

Lauren Bacall

Without imagination, there is no goodness, no wisdom.

Marie Von Ebner-Eschenbach

Imagination, like a memory, can transform lies to truths.

Cristina Garcia

Imagination is new reality in the process of being created. It represents the part of the existing order that can still grow.

Nancy Hale

Independence

I am my own woman.

Maria Eva Duarte de Peron

Independence is happiness.

Susan B. Anthony

There is not the woman born who desires to eat the bread of dependence, no matter whether it be from the hand of father, husband, or brother; for any one who does so eat her bread places herself in the power of the person from whom she takes it.

Susan B. Anthony

Most women still need a room of their own, and the only way to find it may be outside their own homes.

Germaine Greer

Integrity

Integrity can neither be lost nor concealed nor faked nor quenched nor artificially come by nor outlived nor, I believe, in the long run denied.

Eudora Welty

Integrity is so perishable in the summer months of success.

Vanessa Redgrave

The reputation of a thousand years may be determined by the conduct of one hour.

Japanese proverb

There can be no happiness if the things we believe in are different from the things we do.

Freya Madeline Stark

I put a lot of emphasis on how to treat people. The reason for this is simple. The real success of our personal lives and careers can best be measured by the relationships we have with the people most dear to us – our family, friends, and co-workers. If we fail in this aspect of our lives, no matter how vast our worldly possessions or how high on the corporate ladder we climb, we will have achieved very little.

Mary Kay Ash

A great many people think that polysyllables are a sign of intelligence.

Barbara Walters

It's impossible to be loyal to your family, your friends, your country, and your principles, all at the same time.

Mignon McLaughlin

Trust yourself. Think for yourself. Act for yourself. Speak for yourself. Be yourself. Imitation is suicide.

Marva Collins

Every job is a self-portrait of the person who does it.
Autograph your work with excellence.
Author unknown

Intuition

Because of their age-long training in human relations –
for that is what feminine intuition really is – women have a special
contribution to make to any group enterprise.

Margaret Mead

Intuition is a spiritual faculty and does not explain,
but simply points the way.

Florence Scovel Shinn

Trusting our intuition often saves us from disaster.

Anne Wilson Schaef

I don't believe in intuition. When you get sudden flashes of perception,
it is just the brain working faster than usual. But you've been getting ready to
know it for a long time, and when it comes, you feel you've known it always.

Katherine Anne Porter

Trust your hunches... Hunches are usually based on facts
filed away just below the conscious level.

Joyce Brothers

Instinct is the nose of the mind.

Madame De Girardin

God gave women intuition and femininity. Used properly,
the combination easily jumbles the brain of any man I've ever met.

Farrah Fawcett

J

Jealousy

If you don't realize there is always somebody who knows how to do something better than you, then you don't give proper respect for others' talents.

Hortense Canady

Jealousy is no more than feeling alone against smiling enemies.

Elizabeth Bowen

Jealousy is indeed a poor medium to secure love, but it is a secure medium to destroy one's self-respect. For jealous people, like dope-fiends, stoop to the lowest level and in the end inspire only disgust and loathing.

Emma Goldman

Jealousy had a taste, all right – a bitter and tongue-stinging flavour, like a peach stone.

Dolores Hitchens

If envy were a fever, the entire world would be ill.

Danish Proverb

Jealousy is simply and clearly the fear that you do not have value. Jealousy scans for evidence to prove the point – that others will be preferred and rewarded more than you.

Jennifer James

Jealousy is the most dreadfully involuntary of all sins.

Iris Murdoch

Jealousy in romance is like salt in food. A little can enhance the savour, but too much can spoil the pleasure and, under certain circumstances, can be life-threatening.

Maya Angelou

Envy is a symptom of lack of appreciation of our own uniqueness and self worth. Each of us has something to give that no one else has.
Elizabeth O'Connor

Jealousy is all the fun you think they had...
Erica Jong

Journeys

Travel, instead of broadening the mind, often merely lengthens the conversation.

Elizabeth Drew

Distance doesn't matter: it's only the first step that is difficult.

Marie de Vichy-Chamrond

The world is round, and the place which may seem like the end may also be the beginning.

Ivy Baker Priest

The only aspect of our travels that is interesting to others is disaster.

Martha Gellman

We are so often caught up in our destination that we forget to appreciate the journey, especially the goodness of the people we meet on the way.

Author unknown

Make voyages.
Attempt them.
That's all there is.

Elaine Dundy

Nothing is so awesomely unfamiliar as the familiar that discloses itself at the end of a journey.

Cynthia Ozick

You'll never be disappointed if you always keep an eye on uncharted territory, where you'll be challenged and growing and having fun.

Kirstie Alley

Journey is the reward.

Chinese proverb

Justice

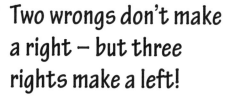

Two wrongs don't make a right – but three rights make a left!

Developing countries may have slightly different concepts of human rights than the West, but it is not cultural imperialism to suggest that women should not be mutilated, enslaved or condemned to die in childbirth.

Nana Agyeman-Rawlings

If we don't stand up for children, then we don't stand for much.

Marian Wright Edelman

The vices of the rich and great are mistaken for error; and those of the poor and lowly, for crimes.

Lady Marguerite Blessington

> No question is ever settled until it is settled right.
>
> *Ella Wheeler Wilcox*

> The likelihood of one individual being right increases in direct ratio to the intensity with which others try to prove him wrong.
>
> *Leonore Fleischer*

> A question that has been raised more than once and that gives me no inner peace is why did so many nations in the past, and often still now, treat women as inferior to men? Everyone can agree how unjust this is, but that is not enough for me. I would also like to know the cause of the great injustice... It is stupid enough of women to have borne it all in silence for such a long time, since the more centuries this arrangement lasts, the more deeply rooted it becomes... Many people, particularly women, but also men, now realize for how long this state of affairs has been wrong, and modern women demand the right of complete independence! But that's not all, respect for women, that's going to have to come as well!
>
> *Anne Frank*

K

Kindness

When you are kind to someone in trouble, you hope they'll remember and be kind to someone else. And, it'll become like a wildfire.

Whoppi Goldberg

If you stop to be kind, you must swerve often from your path.

Mary Webb

Let no one come to you without leaving better and happier. Be the living expression of God's kindness: kindness in your face, kindness in your eyes, and kindness in your smile.

Mother Teresa

Being nice is one of many bridges on the road to happiness.

Donna A. Favors

It's nice to be important, but it's more important to be nice.

Author unknown

Thank you to all the people in the world who are always 10 per cent kinder than they need to be. That's what really makes the world go round.

Helen Exley

Kisses

Nobody wants to kiss when they are hungry.

Dorothy Dix

The kiss originated when the first male reptile licked the first female reptile, implying in a subtle, complimentary way that she was as succulent as the small reptile he had for dinner the night before.

Source unknown

The social kiss is an exchange of insincerity between two combatants on the field of social advancement. It places hygiene before affection and condescension before all else.

Source unknown

A kiss can be a comma, a question mark or an exclamation point. That's basic spelling that every woman ought to know.

Jeanne Bourgeois

A kiss that speaks volumes is seldom a first edition.

Clare Whiting

A kiss without a hug is like a flower without the fragrance.

Author unknown

Happiness is like a kiss – it feels best when you give it to someone else.

Author unknown

Knowledge

If we would have new knowledge, we must get a whole world of new questions.

Susanne K. Langer

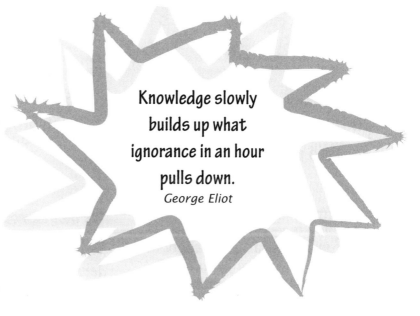

Knowledge slowly builds up what ignorance in an hour pulls down.

George Eliot

Knowledge is essential to conquest; only according to our ignorance are we helpless.

Anne Besant

Well, knowledge is a fine thing, and mother Eve thought so; but she smarted so severely for hers, that most of her daughters have been afraid of it since.

Abigail Adams

It is important to use all knowledge ethically, humanely and lovingly.

Carol Pearson

To appear to be on the inside and know more than others about what is going on is a great temptation for most people. It is a rare person who is willing to seem to know less than he does.

Eleanor Roosevelt

There comes a time when we aren't allowed not to know.

Judith Viorst

Knowledge is much like dust – it sticks to one, one does not know how.

L.E. Landon

In much knowledge there is also much grief.

Queen Marie of Romania

The only man who knows just what he thinks at the present moment is the man who hasn't done any new thinking in the past ten years.

Susan Glaspell

I was brought up to believe that the only thing worth doing was to add to the sum of accurate information in this world.

Margaret Mead

I am not wise. Not knowing, and learning to be comfortable with not knowing, is a great discovery.

Sue Bender

The fact is, women are in chains, and their servitude is all the more debasing because they do not realize it.

Susan B. Anthony

Brass shines as fair to the ignorant as gold to the goldsmith.

Elizabeth I

L

Laughter

Something special happens when people laugh together over something genuinely funny, and not hurtful to anyone. It's like a magic rain that showers down feelings of comfort, safety and belonging to a group.

Mary Jane Belfie

He who laughs, lasts!
Mary Pettibone Poole

Laughter is the lightning rod of play, the eroticism of conversation.

Eva Hoffman

There comes a time when suddenly you realize that laughter is something you remember and that you were the one laughing.

Marlene Dietrich

He who laughs last didn't get it.
Helen Giangregorio

There can never be enough said of the virtues, the dangers, the power of a shared laugh.

Francoise Sagan

Laughter is by definition healthy.
Doris Lessing

A good time for laughing is when you can.

Jessamyn West

A laugh is a terrible weapon.
Kate O'Brien

The head thinks, the hands labour, but it's the heart that laughs.

Liz Curtis Higgs

ha ha-very good!
oh go on then take
the silver!

Laughter springs from the lawless part of our nature.

Agnes Repplier

It's possible to forgive someone a great deal if he makes you laugh.

Caroline Llewellyn

It was the kind of laughter that caught like briars in her chest and felt very much like pain.

Katherine Paterson

There is always a secret irritation about a laugh into which we cannot join.

Agnes Repplier

The laughter of adults was always very different from the laughter of children. The former indicated a recognition of the familiar, but in children it came from the shock of the new.

Elizabeth Hardwick

We have to laugh.
Because laughter, we already know,
is the first evidence of freedom.

Rosario Castellanos

Leadership

I suppose that leadership at one time meant muscle; but today it means getting along with people.

Indira Gandhi

A leader who doesn't hesitate before he sends his nation into battle is not fit to be a leader.

Golda Meir

A leader leads by example, whether he intends to or not.

Author unknown

The minute a person whose word means a great deal to others dares to take the open-hearted and courageous way, many others follow.

Marian Anderson

The secret of a leader lies in the tests he has faced over the whole course of his life and the habit of action he develops in meeting those tests.

Gail Sheehy

Whoever is providing leadership needs to be as fresh and thoughtful and reflective as possible to make the very best fight.

Faye Wattleton

Times of upheaval require not just more leadership but more leaders. People at all organizational levels, whether anointed or self-appointed, must be empowered to share leadership responsibilities.

Rosalynn Carter

Learning

Learning is not attained by chance; it must be sought for with ardour and attended to with diligence.

Abigail Adams

I am learning all the time. The tombstone will be my diploma.

Eartha Kitt

Learning from experience is a faculty almost never practiced.

Barbara Tuchman

It seems that we learn lessons when we least expect them but always when we need them the most, and, the true gift in these lessons always lies in the learning process itself.

Cathy Lee Crosby

A single conversation with a wise man is better than ten years of study.

Chinese proverb

By the time your life is finished, you will have learned just enough to begin it well.

Eleanor Marx

Learn as much as you can while you are young, since life becomes too busy later.

Dana Stewart Scott

You can learn new things at any time in your life if you're willing to be a beginner. If you actually learn to like being a beginner, the whole world opens up to you.

Barbara Sher

Leisure

There is no pleasure in having nothing to do; the fun is in having lots to do – and not doing it.

Mary Wilson Little

Leisure requires the evidence of our own feelings, because it is not so much a quality of time as a peculiar state of mind... What being at leisure means is more easily felt than defined.

Vernon Lee

People would have more leisure time if it weren't for all the leisure-time activities that use it up.

Peg Bracken

People who know how to employ themselves, always find leisure moments, while those who do nothing are forever in a hurry.

Marie-Jeanne Roland

It is in his pleasure that a man really lives; it is from his leisure that he constructs the true fabric of self.

Agnes Repplier

Leisure and the cultivation of human capacities are inextricably interdependent.

Margaret Mead

What we lack is not so much leisure to do as time to reflect and time to feel. What we seldom take is time to experience the things that have happened, the things that are happening, the things that are still ahead of us.

Margaret Mead and Rhoda Metraux

How many inner resources one needs to tolerate a life of leisure without fatigue.

Natalie Clifford Barney

Life

People don't live nowadays: they get about 10 per cent out of life.

Isadora Duncan

Life is just a blank slate, what matters most is what you write on it.

Christine Frankland

Life for both sexes… is arduous, difficult, a perpetual struggle. It calls for gigantic courage and strength. More than anything perhaps, it calls for confidence in one's self. Without self confidence we are as babes in the cradle.

Virginia Woolf, A Room of One's Own

Real life isn't always going to be perfect or go our way, but the recurring acknowledgement of what is working in our lives can help us not only to survive but surmount our difficulties.

Sarah Ban Breathnach

Life is not measured by the number of breaths we take, but by the moments that take our breath away.

Author unknown

Life is an escalator: You can move forward or backward; you can not remain still.

Patricia Russell-McCloud

Life is my college. May I graduate well, and earn some honours!

Louisa May Alcott

Life is like an ever-shifting kaleidoscope – a slight change, and all patterns alter.

Sharon Salzberg

An ABC of Life

Although things are not perfect
Because of trial or pain
Continue in thanksgiving
Do not begin to blame
Even when the times are hard
Fierce winds are bound to blow
God is forever able
Hold on to what you know
Imagine life without His love
Joy would cease to be
Keep thanking Him for all the things
Love imparts to thee
Move out of "Camp Complaining"
No weapon that is known
On earth can yield the power
Praise can do alone
Quit looking at the future
Redeem the time at hand
Start every day with worship
To "thank" is a command
Until we see Him coming
Victorious in the sky
We'll run the race with gratitude
Xalting God most high
Yes, there'll be good times and yes some will be bad, but…
Zion waits in glory… where none are ever sad

Author unknown
From the internet

Life shrinks or expands in proportion to one's courage.

Anais Nin

The game of life is the game of boomerangs. Our thoughts, deeds and words return to us sooner or later, with astounding accuracy.

Florence Scovel Shinn

There is no shortage of good days. It is good lives that are hard to come by.

Annie Dillard

Life is real... So many forget to get real with it.

Donna A. Favors

The point of life is not to succeed...The point of life is to die trying.

Edna St Vincent Millay

Life itself is the proper binge.

Julia Child

Life is like a blanket too short. You pull it up and your toes rebel, you yank it down and shivers meander about your shoulder; but cheerful folks manage to draw their knees up and pass a very comfortable night.

Marion Howard

Life would be so wonderful if we only knew what to do with it.

Greta Garbo

Life never becomes a habit to me. It's always a marvel.

Katherine Mansfield

Life ought to be a struggle of desire towards adventures whose nobility will fertilize the soul.

Rebecca West

Fortunately, psychoanalysis is not the only way to resolve inner conflicts. Life itself remains a very effective therapist.

Karen Horney

Listening

It takes a disciplined person to listen to convictions which are different from their own.

Dorothy Fuldman

The less you talk, the more you are listened to.

Abigail van Buren

Listening, not imitation, may be the sincerest form of flattery.

Dr Joyce Brothers

Know when to tune out. If you listen to too much advice, you may wind up making other people's mistakes.

Ann Landers

If someone listens, or stretches out a hand, or whispers a word of encouragement, or attempts to understand a lonely person, extraordinary things begin to happen.

Loretta Girzartis

To meet at all, one must open ones eyes to another; and there is no true conversation no matter how many words are spoken, unless the eye, unveiled and listening, opens itself to the other.

Jessamyn West

The older I grow the more I listen to people who don't talk much.

Germain G.Glien

Change happens by listening and then starting a dialogue with the people who are doing something you don't believe is right.

Jane Goodall

Loneliness

> ## Loneliness is the most terrible poverty.
> *Mother Teresa*

Only in a house where one has learnt to be lonely does one have (this) solicitude for things. One's relation to them, the daily seeing or touching, begins to become love, and to lay one open to pain.

Elizabeth Bowen

Nobody has ever before asked the nuclear family to live all by itself in a box the way we do. With no relatives, no support, we've put it in an impossible situation.

Margaret Mead

The best remedy for those who are afraid, lonely or unhappy is to go outside, somewhere where they can be quiet, alone with the heavens, nature and God.

Anne Frank

Loneliness is never more cruel than when it is felt in close proximity with someone who has ceased to communicate.

Germaine Greer

The gift of loneliness is sometimes a radical vision of society or one's people that has not previously been taken into account.

Alice Walker

Love

Love involves a peculiar unfathomable combination of understanding and misunderstanding.

Diane Arbus

Love is a great beautifier.

Louisa May Alcott

If love does not know how to give and take without restrictions, it is not love, but a transaction that never fails to lay stress on a plus and a minus.

Emma Goldman

Love is an exploding cigar we willingly smoke.

Lynda Barry

Love is like dew that falls on both nettles and lilies.

Swedish proverb

Love is a fruit in season at all times, and within reach of every hand.

Mother Teresa

Love makes your soul crawl out from its hiding place.

Zora Neale Hurston

There's nothing more freeing than the shackles of love.

Emma Racine deFleur

Love is the only shocking act left on the face of the earth.

Sarah Bernhard

Hate leaves ugly scars, love leaves beautiful ones.

Mignon McLaughlin

I only want to love once, but I want to love everybody for the rest of my life.

Lauren Ford

If you have love in your life, it can make up for a great many things that are missing. If you don't have love in your life, no matter what else there is, it's not enough.

Ann Landers

M

Marriage

When two people marry they become in the eyes of the law one person, and that one person is the husband!

Shana Alexander

Intimacy is what makes a marriage, not a ceremony, not a piece of paper from the state.

Kathleen Norris

A real marriage bears no resemblance to those marriages of interest and ambition. It is two lovers who live together.

Lady Mary Wortley Montagu

The real act of marriage takes place in the heart, not in the ballroom or church or synagogue. It's a choice you make – not just on your wedding day, but over and over again – and that choice is reflected in the way you treat your husband or wife.

Barbara De Angelis

A wife who meets you halfway, who challenges you when you need it and even when you don't, who isn't afraid to express herself when she disagrees with you is the stuff of a lively and living marriage.

Gayle Roper

Marriage is not just spiritual communion; it is also remembering to take out the trash.

Joyce Brothers

> Marriage is a bit like discovering a continent. Much of it is mapped out – you can see the coastline and the mountains – but a lot is akin to what Christopher Columbus must have felt when he was searching for America: he knew it was there, but had no idea how to fill in the detail.
>
> *Elizabeth Buchan*

Every marriage is happy. It's the living together afterwards that's the challenge

Anne Landers

Love is supposed to start with bells ringing and go downhill from there. But it was the opposite for me. There's an intense connection between us, and as we stayed together, the bells rang louder.

Lisa Niemi

Maturity

Maturity is the time of life when, if you had the time, you'd have the time of your life.

Author unknown

One does not get better but different and older and that is always a pleasure.

Gertrude Stein

Maturity isn't a product of growing older. It's a product of growing wiser.

Ann Landers

If growing up is the process of creating ideas and dreams about what life should be, then maturity is letting go again.

Mary Beth Danielson

I believe the sign of maturity is accepting deferred gratification.

Peggy Cahn

Maturity: Be able to stick with a job until it is finished. Be able to bear an injustice without having to get even. Be able to carry money without spending it. Do your duty without being supervised.

Ann Landers

Memory/Memories

Memory is the diary we all carry about with us.

Mary H. Waldrip

Some memories are realities, and are better than anything that can ever happen to one again.

Willa Sibert Cather

Memory is a magnet. It will pull to it and hold only material that nature has designed it to attract.

Jessamyn West

Memory – the very skin of life.

Elizabeth Hardwick

I can understand that memory must be selective, else it would choke on the glut of experience. What I cannot understand is why it selects what it does.

Virgilia Peterson

I wear the key of memory, and can open every door in the house of my life.

Amelia E. Barr

I remember what was missing instead of what was there. I am a chronicler of absence.

Carrie Fisher

In memory each of us is an artist: each of us creates.

Patricia Hampl

The hills of one's youth are all mountains.

Mari Sandoz

Memory is a complicated thing, a relative to truth, but not its twin.

Barbara Kingsolver

Looking repeatedly into the past, you do not necessarily become fascinated with your own life, but rather with the phenomenon of memory.

Patricia Hampl

I think, myself, that one's memories represent those moments which, insignificant as they may seem, nevertheless represent the inner self and oneself as most really oneself.

Agatha Christie

Memories are like corks left out of bottles. They swell. They no longer fit.

Harriet Doerr

The irony of life is not that you cannot forget but that you can.

Gertrude Atherton

Just remember enough never to be vulnerable again: total forgetting could be as self-destructive as complete remembering.

Helen MacInnes

I have a terrible memory;
I never forget a thing.

Edith Konecky

How we remember, what we remember, and why we remember form the most personal map of our individuality.

Christina Baldwin

I can never remember things I didn't understand in the first place.

Amy Tan

Memory is to love what the saucer is to the cup.

Elizabeth Bowen

Men

A lot of guys think the larger a woman's breasts are, the less intelligent she is. I don't think it works like that. I think it's the opposite. I think the larger a woman's breasts are, the less intelligent the men become.

Anita Wise

You have to be very fond of men. Very, very fond. You have to be very fond of them to love them. Otherwise they're simply unbearable.

Marguerite Duras

A great man leaves clean work behind him, and requires no sweeper up of the chips.

Elizabeth Barret Browning

Men define intelligence, men define usefulness, men tell us what is beautiful, men even tell us what is womanly.

Sally Kempton

Men were made for war. Without it they wandered greyly about, getting under the feet of the women, who were trying to organize the really important things of life.

Alice Thomas Ellis

Men love putting women on a pedestal because it's so much more satisfying when they knock them off. They fall farther.

Clare Booth Luce

The only time a woman really succeeds in changing a man is when he's a baby.

Natalie Wood

You see a lot of smart guys with dumb women, but you hardly ever see a smart woman with a dumb guy.

Erica Jong

The world men inhabit is rather bleak. It is a world full of doubt and confusion, where vulnerability must be hidden, not shared; where competition, not co-operation, is the order of the day; where men sacrifice the possibility of knowing their own children and sharing in their upbringing, for the sake of a job they may have chosen by chance, which may not suit them and which in many cases dominates their lives to the exclusion of much else.

Anna Ford

It is no use blaming the men – we made them what they are – and now it is up to us to try and make ourselves – the makers of men – a little more responsible.

Nancy Astor

Men aren't the way they are because they want to drive women crazy; they've been trained to be that way for thousands of years. And that training makes it very difficult for men to be intimate.

Barbara De Angelis

Men and Women

A successful man is one who makes more money than his wife can spend. A successful woman is one who can find such a man.

Lana Turner

The great truth is that women actually like men, and men can never believe it.

Isabel Paterson

When a woman is very, very bad, she is awful, but when a man is correspondingly good, he is weird.

Minna Antrim

Because of our social circumstances, male and female are really two cultures and their life experiences are utterly different.

Kate Millet

The test of a man is how well he is able to feel about what he thinks. The test of a woman is how well she is able to think about what she feels.

Mary Mcdowell

Boys will be boys, but girls will be women.

Author unknown

One of my theories is that men love with their eyes; women love with their ears.

Zsa Zsa Gabor

Women have got to make the world safe for men since men have made it so darned unsafe for women.

Lady Nancy Astor

The woman's vision is deep reaching, the man's far reaching. With the man the world is his heart, with the woman the heart is her world.

Betty Grable

Mercy

The heart has always the pardoning power.

Madame Anne Sophie Swetchine

We hand folks over to God's mercy, and show none ourselves.

George Eliot

Difficult as it is really to listen to someone in affliction; it is just as difficult for him to know that compassion is listening to him.

Simone Weil

We all need the waters of the Mercy River. Though they don't run deep, there's usually enough, just enough, for the extravagance of our lives.

Joan Agee

Nothing in this low and ruined world bears the meek impress of the Son of God so surely as forgiveness.

Alice Cary

Miracles

When there is great love there are always miracles.

Willa Sibert Cather

I think miracles exist in part as gifts and in part as clues that there is something beyond the flat world we see.

Peggy Noonan

The miracles of nature do not seem miracles because they are so common. If no one had ever seen a flower, even a dandelion would be the most startling event in the world.

Author unknown

The capacity to give one's attention to a sufferer is a very rare and difficult thing; it is almost a miracle; it is a miracle.

Simone Weil

We are miracles. Each of us is an absolute astonishment. So whether you believe in miracles or not, we still are. We still partake of miracledom.

Ruby Doe

Miracles occur naturally as expressions of love. The real miracle is the love that inspires them. In this sense everything that comes from love is a miracle.

Marianne Williamson

After all, I don't see why I am always asking for private, individual, selfish miracles when every year there are miracles like white dogwood.

Anne Morrow Lindbergh

Misery

Just because you are miserable doesn't mean you can't enjoy your life.

Dr Annette Goodheart

You can't be brave if you've only had wonderful things happen to you.

Mary Tyler Moore

Friends love misery, in fact. Sometimes, especially if we are too lucky or too successful or too pretty, our misery is the only thing that endears us to our friends.

Erica Jong

Misery is a communicable disease.

Martha Graham

Let your tears come. Let them water your soul.

Eileen Mayhew

I don't think of all the misery but of the beauty that still remains.

Anne Frank

Nobody really cares if you're miserable, so you might as well be happy.

Cynthia Nelms

Mistakes

Mistakes are the usual bridge between inexperience and wisdom.

Phyllis Therous

It's not the mistakes, but how you react to the mistakes that makes the difference.

Julie Wainwright

It is not easy, but you have to be willing to make mistakes. And the earlier you make those mistakes, the better.

Jane Cahill Pfeiffer

Mistakes are part of the dues one pays for a full life.

Sophia Loren

Be aware that young people have to be able to make their own mistakes and that times change.

Gina Shapira

Errors look so very ugly in persons of small means – one feels they are taking quite a liberty in going astray; whereas people of fortune may naturally indulge in a few delinquencies.

George Eliot

Learn from the mistakes of others – you can never live long enough to make them all yourself.

Author unknown

~~~~~~~~~~~~~~~~~~~~~~~~~~~

Modesty

It is far more impressive when others discover your good qualities without your help.

'Miss Manners'

Modesty: the gentle art of enhancing your charm by pretending not to be aware of it.

Author unknown

Conceit spoils the finest genius. There is not much danger that real talent or goodness will be overlooked long; even if it is, the consciousness of possessing and using it well should satisfy one, and the great charm of all power is modesty.

Louisa May Alcott

Modesty is the chastity of merit, the virginity of noble souls.

Madame de Girardin

Fidelity to conscience is inconsistent with retiring modesty. If it be so, let the modesty succumb. It can be only a false modesty which can be thus endangered.

Harriet Martineau

Money

People don't have fortunes left them in that style nowadays; men have to work and women to marry for money. It's a dreadfully unjust world.

Louisa May Alcott

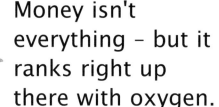

Money isn't everything – but it ranks right up there with oxygen.

Rita Davenport

If all the rich people in the world divided up their money among themselves there wouldn't be enough to go round.

Christina Stead

I have enough money to last me the rest of my life, unless I buy something.

Jackie Mason

Money is a burden. All anybody needs is enough to eat and a roof over their heads. Any more than that is stress.

Shania Twain (Singer, who earned £30 million in 2004)

Every time you spend money, you're casting a vote for the kind of world you want.

Anna Lappe

If you want to know what God thinks of money, just look at the people he gave it to.

Dorothy Parker

Thou shouldst not become presumptuous through much treasure and wealth; for in the end it is necessary for thee to leave all.

Zsa Zsa Gabor

No one would remember the Good Samaritan if he'd only had good intentions – he had money, too.

Margaret Thatcher

We can tell our values by looking at our cheque book stubs.

Gloria Steinem

The only way not to think about money is to have a great deal of it.

Edith Wharton

People who think money can do anything may very well be suspected of doing anything for money.

Mary Pettibone Poole

What I know about money, I learned the hard way - by having had it.

Margaret Halsey

Nothing that costs only a dollar is not worth having.

Elizabeth Arden

I must say I hate money, but it's the lack of it that I hate most.

Katherine Mansfield

Some couples go over their budgets very carefully every month, others just go over them.

Sally Poplin

Some people think they are worth a lot of money just because they have it.

Fannie Hurst

Money speaks sense in a language all nations understand.

Aphra Behn

So you think that money is the root of all evil? Have you ever asked what is the root of money?

Ayn Rand

Money can be more of a barrier between people than language or race or religion.

Vera Caspary

The best way to attract money, she had discovered, was to give the appearance of having it.

Gail Sheehy

As soon as you bring up money, I notice, conversation gets sociological, then political, then moral.

Kate Smiley

Money isn't everything, your health is the other 10 per cent.

Lillian Day

It is true that money attracts; but much money repels.

Cynthia Ozick

Friends and good manners will carry you where money won't go.

Margaret Walker

I make money using my brains and lose money listening to my heart. But in the long run my books balance pretty well.

Kate Seredy

Money dignifies what is frivolous if unpaid for.

Virginia Woolf

Money is of value for what it buys, and in love it buys time, place, intimacy, comfort, and a private corner alone.

Mae West

Mothers

The formative period for building character for eternity is in the nursery. The mother is queen of that realm and sways a sceptre more potent than that of kings or priests.

Author unknown

A Freudian slip is when you say one thing but mean your mother.

Author unknown

Women who miscalculate are called mothers.

Abigail Van Buren

A daughter is a mother's gender partner, her closest ally in the family confederacy, an extension of herself. And mothers are their daughters' role model, their biological and emotional road map, the arbiter of all their relationships.

Victoria Secunda

I cannot forget my mother. She is my bridge. When I needed to get across, she steadied herself long enough for me to run across safely.

Renita Weems

Mothers are the most instinctive philosophers.

Harriet Beecher Stowe

Mother love is the fuel that enables a normal human being to do the impossible.

Marion C. Garretty

[A] mother is one to whom you hurry when you are troubled.

Emily Dickinson

Our mothers always remain the strangest, craziest people we've ever met.

Marguerite Duras

A mother is never cocky or proud, because she knows the school principal may call at any minute to report that her child has just driven a motorcycle through the gymnasium.

Mary Kay Blakeley

Instant availability without continuous presence is probably the best role a mother can play.

Lotte Bailyn

Motherhood

Motherhood has a very humanizing effect. Everything gets reduced to essentials.

Meryl Streep

Motherhood is too rewarding and too absorbing an occupation to be handed over lightly.

Sigrid Rausing

Sometimes the strength of motherhood is greater than natural laws.

Barbara Kingsolver

I got a lot more done than most people by five because I knew I had to be home for my children.

Meg Whitman

Motherhood is priced of God, at price no man may dare to lessen or misunderstand.

Helen Hunt Jackson

Being a full-time mother is one of the highest salaried jobs in my field, since the payment is pure love.

Mildred B. Vermont

In my experience most mothers feel guilty – whether they work outside the home or inside the home. If you can free yourself from this useless harmful emotion, your life will be happier and more productive, and your children's lives will be too.

Rebecca Matthias

No culture on earth outside of mid-century suburban America has ever deployed one woman per child without simultaneously assigning her such major productive activities as weaving, farming, gathering, temple maintenance and tent-building. The reason is that full-time, one-on-one child-raising is not good for women or children.

Barbara Ehrenreich

By and large, mothers and housewives are the only workers who do not have regular time off. They are the great vacationless class.

Anne Morrow Lindbergh

Women know the way to rear up children (to be just). They know a simple, merry, tender knack of tying sashes, fitting baby-shoes, and stringing pretty words that make no sense and kissing full sense into empty words.

Elizabeth Barrett Browning

For that's what a woman, a mother wants – to teach her children to take an interest in life. She knows it's safer for them to be interested in other people's happiness than to believe in their own.

Marguerite Duras

Maternity is on the face of it an unsociable experience. The selfishness that a woman has learned to stifle or to dissemble where she alone is concerned, blooms freely and unashamed on behalf of her offspring.

Emily James Putnam

Society has a tremendous stake in insisting on a woman's natural fitness for the career of mother: the alternatives are all too expensive.

Ann Oakley

Men never think, at least seldom think, what a hard task it is for us women to go through this very often. God's will be done, and if He decrees that we are to have a great number of children, why, we must try to bring them up as useful and exemplary members of society.

Queen Victoria

N

Nature

The best remedy for those who are afraid, lonely or unhappy is to go outside, somewhere where they can be quiet, alone with the heavens, nature and God. Because only then does one feel that all is as it should be and that God wishes to see people happy, amidst the simple beauty of nature. As long as this exists, and it certainly always will, I know that then there will always be comfort for every sorrow, whatever the circumstances may be. And I firmly believe that nature brings solace in all troubles.

Anne Frank

Nature, like us, is sometimes caught without her diadem.

Emily Dickinson

Meanings, moods, the whole scale of our inner experience finds in nature the correspondence through which we may know our boundless selves.

Kathleen Raine

Nature has been for me, for as long as I remember, a source of solace, inspiration, adventure and delight; a home, a teacher, a companion.

Lorraine Anderson

To sit in the shade on a fine day and look upon verdure is the most perfect refreshment.

Jane Austen

Nature has no mercy at all. Nature says, I'm going to snow. If you have on a bikini and no snowshoes, that's tough. I am going to snow anyway.

Maya Angelou

Neighbours

Sometimes a neighbour whom we have disliked a lifetime for his arrogance and conceit lets fall a single commonplace remark that shows us another side, another man, really; a man uncertain and puzzled and in the dark like ourselves.

Willa Cather

Hedges between keep friendships green.

Proverb

Love thy neighbour as thyself, but choose thy neighbourhood.

Louise Beal

To act the part of a true friend requires more conscientious feeling than to fill with credit and complacency any other station or capacity in social life.

Mrs Sarah Stickney Ellis

The love of our neighbour in all its fullness simply means being able to say, "What are you going through?"

Simone Weil

With regard to the choice of friends, there is little to say; for a friend is never chosen. A secret sympathy, the attraction of a thousand nameless qualities, a charm in the expression of the countenance, even in the voice or manner, a similarity of circumstances – these are the things that begin attachment.

Mrs Anna Letitia Barbauld

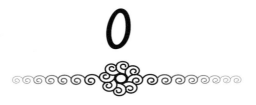

O

Obstacles

Never accept 'No'. Things change – in the environment, in people's perceptions, and the situation – so always seek the angles that move you towards your goal.

Rose Marie Bravo

When you struggle, that's when you realize what you're made of, and that's when you realize what the people around you can do. You learn who you'd want to take with you to a war, and who you'd only want to take to lunch.

Chamique Holdsclaw

In most cases the only thing holding people back is themselves.

Candice Carpenter

All that is necessary to break the spell of inertia and frustration is this: Act as if it were impossible to fail. That is the talisman, the formula, the command of right-about-face which turns us from failure towards success.

Dorothea Brande

Obstacles often are not personal attacks; they are muscle builders.

Anne Wilson Schaef

Never say 'never' – for if you live long enough, the chances are you will not be able to abide by its restrictions. Never is a long, undependable time, and life is too full of rich possibilities to have restrictions placed upon it.

Gloria Swanson

To fly,
we have to
have
resistance.
Maya Lin

When people keep telling you that you can't do a thing, you kind of like to try it.

Margaret Fuller

To tell a woman everything she may not do is to tell her what she can do.

Spanish proverb

Opinion

Speak your mind – even if your voice shakes. Well-aimed slingshots can topple giants.

Maggie Kuhn

A man is getting along on the road to wisdom when he begins to realize that his opinion is just an opinion.

Author unknown

We must preserve our right to think and differ.

Eleanor Roosevelt

We must not allow other people's limited perceptions to define us.

Virginia Satir

I usually make up my mind about a man in ten seconds, and I very rarely change it.

Margaret Thatcher

Opinions are the cheapest commodities in the world.

Author unknown

The important thing is not what they think of me, but what I think of them.

Queen Victoria

Opinions are formed in a process of open discussion and public debate, and where no opportunity for the forming of opinions exists, there may be moods — moods of the masses and moods of individuals, the latter no less fickle and unreliable than the former — but no opinion.

Hannah Arendt

Opportunity

Great opportunities to help others seldom come, but small ones surround us everyday.

Sally Koch

Security is not the meaning of my life. Great opportunities are worth the risk.

Shirley Hufstedler

There are so many doors to be opened, and I'm not afraid to look behind them.

Elizabeth Taylor

Grasp your opportunities, no matter how poor your health; nothing is worse for your health than boredom.

Mignon McLaughlin

Nothing is so often irretrievably missed as a daily opportunity.

Marie von Ebner-Eschenbach

Don't sit down and wait for the opportunities to come; you have to get up and make them.

Madame C. J. Walker

There is no object that we see; no action that we do; no good that we enjoy; no evil that we feel, or fear, but we may make some spiritual advantage of all: and [s]he that makes such improvement is wise, as well as pious.

Anne Bradstreet

With increased opportunity comes increased stress. The stress comes from multiple conflicting demands and very little in the way of role models.

Madeline Hemmings

One can present people with opportunities. One cannot make them equal to them.

Rosamond Lehmann

Oppression

Oppression that is clearly inexorable and invincible does not give rise to revolt but to submission.

Simone Weil

You may try but you can never imagine what it is to have a man's form of genius in you, and to suffer the slavery of being a girl.

George Eliot

I have never been contained except I made the prison.

Mari Evans

As long as you keep a person down, some part of you has to be down there to hold him down, so it means you cannot soar as you otherwise might.

Marian Anderson

All oppression creates a state of war.

Simone De Beauvoir

Human beings are so made that the ones who do the crushing feel nothing; it is the person crushed who feels what is happening. Unless one has placed oneself on the side of the oppressed, to feel with them, one cannot understand.

Simone Weil

Organization

It takes as much energy to wish as it does to plan.

Eleanor Roosevelt

A schedule defends from chaos and whim. It is a net for catching days. It is a scaffolding on which a worker can stand and labour with both hands at sections of time. A schedule is a mock-up of reason and order – willed, faked, and so brought into being.

Anne Dillard

The trouble with organizing a thing is that pretty soon folks get to paying more attention to the organization than to what they're organized for.

Laura Ingalls Wilder

To know where you can find a thing is the chief part of learning.

Author unknown

We have created trouble for ourselves in organizations by confusing control with order.

Margaret J. Wheatley

Early in my career I felt that organization would destroy my creativity. Whereas now, I feel the opposite. Discipline is the concrete that allows you to be creative.

Verna Gibson

Don't agonize. Organize.

Florence Kennedy

Originality

You've gotta be original, because if you're like someone else, what do they need you for?

Bernadette Peters

True originality consists not in a new manner but in a new vision.

Edith Wharton

If you are going to be original, you are going to be wrong a lot.

Author unknown

Originality is... a by-product of sincerity.

Marianne Moore

There are no original ideas. There are only original people.

Barbara Grizzuli Harrison

Set me a task in which I can put something of my very self, and it is a task no longer. It is joy and art.

Bliss Carman

Success is creating something original and lasting – whether it is a company, a work of art, an idea or analysis that influences others, or a happy and productive family.

Linda Chevez

P

Parenthood

It kills you to see them grow up. But I guess it would kill you quicker if they didn't.

Barbara Kingsolver

It's not only children who grow. Parents do too. As much as we watch to see what our children do with their lives, they are watching us to see what we do with ours. I can't tell my children to reach for the sun. All I can do is reach for it myself.

Joyce Maynard

Parenthood: That state of being better chaperoned than you were before marriage.

Marcelene Cox

A wise parent humours the desire for independent action, so as to become the friend and advisor when his absolute rule shall cease.

Elizabeth Gaskell

I take a very practical view of raising children. I put a sign in each of their rooms: Checkout Time is 18 years.

Erma Bombeck

Perhaps the best function of parenthood is to teach the young creature to love with safety, so that it may be able to venture unafraid when later emotion comes; the thwarting of the instinct to love is the root of all sorrow and not sex only but divinity itself is insulted when it is repressed.

Freya Stark

It would seem that something which means poverty, disorder and violence every single day should be avoided entirely, but the desire to beget children is a natural urge.

Phyllis Diller

The word No carries a lot more meaning when spoken by a parent who also knows how to say Yes.

Joyce Maynard

I wish you would moderate that fondness you have for your children. I do not mean you should abate any part of your care, or not do your duty to them in its utmost extent, but I would have you early prepare yourself for disappointments, which are heavy in proportion to their being surprising.

Lady Mary Wortley Montagu

It's frightening to think that you mark your children merely by being yourself. It seems unfair. You can't assume the responsibility for everything you do – or don't do.

Simone De Beauvoir

Passion

A passionate interest in what you do is the secret of enjoying life – whether it is helping old people or children, or making cheese or growing earthworms.

Julia Childs

My passions were all gathered together like fingers that made a fist. Drive is considered aggression today; I knew it then as purpose.

Bette Davis

I'm very determined and stubborn. There's a desire in me that makes me want to do more and more, and to do it right. Each one of us has a fire in our heart for something. It's our goal in life to find it and to keep it lit.

Mary Lou Retton

There's no blameless life save for the passionless.

George Eliot

The fiery moments of passionate experience are the moments of wholeness and totality of the personality.

Anais Nin

Find ecstasy in life; the mere sense of living is joy enough.

Emily Dickinson

How little do they know human nature, who think they can say to passion, so far shalt thou go, and no farther!

Sarah Scott

Past

Each has his past shut in him like the leaves of a book known to him by heart and his friends can only read the title.

Virginia Woolf

One cannot and must not try to erase the past merely because it does not fit the present.

Golda Meir

Clinging to the past is the problem. Embracing change is the answer.

Gloria Steinem

The past is not a package one can lay away.

Emily Dickinson

There is a way to look at the past. Don't hide from it. It will not catch you – if you don't repeat it.

Pearl Bailey

If you're still hanging onto a dead dream of yesterday, laying flowers on its grave by the hour, you cannot be planting the seeds for a new dream to grow today.

Joyce Chapman

People seem to lose all respect for the past; events succeed each other with such velocity that the most remarkable one of a few years gone by, is no more remembered than if centuries had closed over it.

Marguerite Gardiner

The past is strapped to our backs. We do not have to see it; we can always feel it.

Mignon McLaughlin

It's a pleasure to share one's memories. Everything remembered is dear, endearing, touching, precious. At least the past is safe – though we didn't know it at the time. We know it now because it's in the past, because we have survived.

Susan Sontag

Patience

Patience
is bitter, but it's
fruit is sweet.

Lida Clarkson

Do not ask for fulfillment in all your life, but for patience to accept frustration.

Brenda Short

We usually learn to wait only when we have no longer anything to wait for.

Marie Ebner-Eschenbach

Patience is the ability to idle your motor when you feel like stripping your gears.

Barbara Johnson

Sometimes it helps to know that I just can't do it all. One step at a time is all that's possible – even when those steps are taken on the run.

Anne W. Schaef

Patience is the ability to count down before you blast off.

Author unknown

Face your deficiencies and acknowledge them; but do not let them master you. Let them teach you patience, sweetness, insight... When we do the best we can, we never know what miracle is wrought in our life, or in the life of another.

Helen Keller

If we could have a little patience, we should escape much mortification; time takes away as much as it gives.

Madame de Sevigne

Peace

God is a peaceful ground of being. He is the energy of non-violence. To ask Him to help is to ask Him to turn us into profoundly peaceful people.

Marianne Williamson

When you find peace within yourself, you become the kind of person who can live at peace with others.

Peace Pilgrim

Peace is not the absence of conflict but the presence of creative alternatives for responding to conflict – alternatives to passive or aggressive responses, alternatives to violence.

Dorothy Thompson

Ultimately, we have just one moral duty: to reclaim large areas of peace in ourselves, more and more peace, and to reflect it toward others. And the more peace there is in us, the more peace there will also be in our troubled world.

Etty Hillesum

Peace will come wherever it is sincerely invited.

Alice Walker

I do not want peace that passeth all understanding, I want understanding that bringeth peace.

Helen Keller

Let us not be justices of the peace, but angels of peace.

St Theresa of Lisieux

Perfume

Perfume promiscuity is a sign of immaturity. Not deciding on a scent by the time you are 30 should be a cause for concern.

Lesley Thomas

The fragrance always stays in the hand that gives the rose.

Hada Bejar

'Where should one use perfume?' a young woman asked. 'Wherever one wants to be kissed,' I said.

Gabrielle "Coco" Chanel

We all have fragrances left over from childhood – those special smells that, when inhaled, instantly propel us back into the past.

Ronna Snyder

Don't wear perfume in the garden – unless you want to be pollinated by bees.

Anne Raver

Your life leaves behind a fragrance long after you're gone. Make sure it's a sweet one.

Ronna Snyder

The sense of smell, almost more than any other, has the power to recall memories and it is a pity that you use it so little.

Rachel Carson

'Ford Focus?!' what was I thinking? next time I'll splash out for Jaguar!

To attract men, I wear a perfume called 'New Car Interior'.

Rita Rudner

Persistance

Your persistence is your measure of faith in yourself.
Author unknown

You have to have confidence in your ability, and then be tough enough to follow through.
Rosalynn Carter

It's the fight itself that keeps you going.
Sidonie-Gabrielle Collete

If you get up one time more than you fall, you will make it through.
Author unknown

It helps, I think, to consider ourselves on a very long journey: the main thing is to keep to the faith, to endure, to help each other when we stumble or tire, to weep and press on.
Mary Caroline Richards

Just keep swimming, just keep swimming, just keep swimming...
Dory the fish
(from the movie Finding Nemo*)*

When you put your hand to the plough, you can't put it down until you get to the end of the row.
Alice Paul

Don't give up. Keep going. There is always a chance that you will stumble over something terrific. I have never heard of anyone stumbling over anything while he was sitting down.
Ann Landers

Perspective

If you see a whole thing – it seems that it's always beautiful. Planets, lives... But up close a world's all dirt and rocks. And day to day, life's a hard job, you get tired, you lose the pattern.

Ursula Le Guin

I looked always outside of myself to see what I could make the world give me, instead of looking within myself to see what was there.

Belle Livingstone

A pedestal is as much a prison as any small space.

Gloria Steinem

There is no magic in small plans. When I consider my ministry I think of the world. Anything less would not be worthy of Christ, nor of His will for my life.

Henrietta Mears

No object is mysterious. The mystery is your eye.

Elizabeth Bowen

The road that is built in hope is more pleasant to the traveller than the road built in despair, even though they both lead to the same destination.

Marian Zimmer Bradley

We don't see things as they are, we see them as we are.

Anaïs Nin

Eyes of youth have sharp sight, but commonly not so deep as old age.

Elizabeth I

If you're being run out of town, get in front of the crowd and make it look like a parade.

Author unknown

Possessions

The pleasure of possession, whether we possess trinkets, or offspring – or possibly books, or prints, or chessmen, or postage stamps – lies in showing these things to friends who are experiencing no immediate urge to look at them.

Agnes Repplier

Through the years I have found it wonderful to acquire, but it is also wonderful to divest. It's rather like exhaling.

Helen Hayes

Anything you cannot relinquish when it has outlived its usefulness possesses you, and in this materialistic age a great many of us are possessed by our possessions.

Peace Pilgrim

The best things in life aren't things.

Ann Landers

We are all more blind to what we have than to what we have not.

Audre Lorde

If my hands are fully occupied in holding onto something, I can neither give nor receive.

Dorothee Solle

Until you make peace with who you are, you'll never be content with what you have.

Doris Mortman

The things people discard tell more about them than the things they keep.

Hilda Lawrence

All things that a man owns hold him far more than he holds them.

Sigrid Undset

Why grab possessions like thieves, or divide them like socialists when you can ignore them like wise men?

Natalie Clifford Barney

I used to believe that anything was better than nothing. Now I know that sometimes nothing is better.

Glenda Jackson

As for things,
how they do accumulate,
how often I wish to exclaim,
"Oh don't give me that!"
Susan Hale

Possibilities

Set your sights high, the higher the better. Expect the most wonderful things to happen, not in the future but right now. Realize that nothing is too good. Allow absolutely nothing to hamper you or hold you up in any way.

Eileen Caddy

Two people can do anything as long as one of them is the Lord.
Author unknown

I am willing to put myself through anything; temporary pain or discomfort means nothing to me as long as I can see that the experience will take me to a new level. I am interested in the unknown, and the only path to the unknown is through breaking barriers, an often-painful process.

Diana Nyad

She didn't know it couldn't be done, so she went ahead and did it.

Mary S. Almanac

No star is ever lost we once have seen, we always may be what we might have been.

Adelaide Proctor

Potential

Most women don't realize that they've got the stuff and they can move on up.

Marion Sandler

Each of us is gifted with great potential – for wisdom, creativity, love, kindness, compassion, strength and tenderness.

Kristine Carlson

A pint can't hold a quart – if it holds a pint it is doing all that can be expected of it.

Margaret Deland

A sobering thought: what if, at this very moment, I am living up to my full potential?

Jane Wagner

Continuous effort, not strength or intelligence is the key to unlocking our potential.

Liane Cardes

Reach up as far as you can, and God will reach down all the way.

Author unknown

We all have the extraordinary coded within us… waiting to be released.

Jean Houston

Our being is subject to all the chances of life. There are so many things we are capable of, that we could be or do. The potentialities are so great that we never, any of us, are more than one-fourth fulfilled.

Katherine Anne Porter

Poverty

When you have only two pennies left in the world, buy a loaf of bread with one, and a lily with the other.

Chinese proverb

The hardship and suffering caused by unemployment penetrates every area of life. While politicians are tallying up the economic costs of unemployment, I wish they'd be more aware of the social and moral consequences which are unparalleled in many nations today.

Eva Burrows

Our life of poverty is as necessary as the work itself. Only in heaven will we see how much we owe to the poor for helping us to love God better because of them.

Mother Teresa

You lose your manners when you're poor.
Lillian Hellman

You don't seem to realize that a poor person who is unhappy is in a better position than a rich person who is unhappy. Because the poor person has hope. He thinks money would help.

Jean Kerr

The next time you feel like complaining, remember: Your garbage disposal probably eats better than 30 per cent of the people in this world.

Author unknown

I was raised by my parents to believe that it was my obligation to help those with less than I had.

Faye Wattleton

The price of indulging yourself in your youth in the things you cannot afford is poverty and dependence in your old age.

Dorothy Dix

Power

Being powerful is like being a lady. If you have to tell people you are, you aren't.

Margaret Thatcher

Women have been called queens for a long time, but the kingdom given them isn't worth ruling.

Louisa May Alcott

Power can be taken, but not given. The process of the taking is empowerment in itself.

Gloria Steinem

A word after a word after a word is power.

Margaret Atwood

If school results were the key to power, girls would be running the world.

Sarah Boseley

To achieve, you need thought. You have to know what you are doing and that's real power.

Ayn Rand

When I dare to be powerful – to use my strength in the service of my vision, then it becomes less and less important whether I am afraid.

Audre Lorde

Power! Did you ever hear of men being asked whether other souls should have power or not? It is born in them. You may dam up the fountain of water, and make it a stagnant marsh, or you may let it run free and do its work; but you cannot say whether it shall be there; it is there. And it will act, if not openly for good, then covertly for evil; but it will act.

Olive Schreiner

Prayer

Prayer does not use up artificial energy, doesn't burn up any fossil fuel, doesn't pollute. Neither does song, neither does love, neither does the dance.

Margaret Mead

Why is it when we talk to God we're said to be praying, but when God talks to us we're schizophrenic?

Lily Tomlin

Praying without ceasing is not ritualized, nor are there even words. It is a constant state of awareness of oneness with God.

Peace Pilgrim

God speaks in the silence of the heart. Listening is the beginning of prayer.

Mother Teresa

Prayer comes from the heart as simply as a brook runs down to a river. Prayer is simply love gushing towards the beloved.

Catherine de Hueck Doherty

We neither laugh alone, nor weep alone, why then should we pray alone?

Anna Letitia Barbauld

What we usually pray to God is not that His will be done, but that He approve ours.

Helga Bergold Gross

We must move from asking God to take care of the things that are breaking our hearts, to praying about the things that are breaking His heart.

Margaret Gibb

God answers sharp and sudden on some prayers and thrusts the thing we have prayed for in our face, like a gauntlet with a gift in it.

Elizabeth Barrett Browning

Grow flowers of gratitude in the soil of prayer.

Verbena Woods

I have not placed reading before praying because I regard it more important, but because, in order to pray aright, we must understand what we are praying for.

Angelina Grimke

Just pray for a tough hide and a tender heart.

Ruth Graham

I believe in prayer. It's the best way we have to draw strength from heaven.

Josephine Baker

Pray inwardly, even if you do not enjoy it. It does good, though you feel nothing. Yes, even though you think you are doing nothing.

Julian of Norwich

The Present Moment

Make the best of today, for there is no tomorrow until after today.

Liz Strehlow

It's been said that there are two days over which we have no control: yesterday, because it's a cancelled cheque, and tomorrow, because it's a promissory note.

Diane Conway

One day at a time – this is enough. Do not look back and grieve over the past, for it is gone; and do not be troubled about the future, for it has not yet come. Live in the present, and make it so beautiful that it will be worth remembering.

Ida Scott Taylor

Yesterday is history, tomorrow is a mystery and today is a gift; that's why they call it the present.

Eleanor Roosevelt

Each moment in time we have it all, even when we think we don't.

Melody Beattie

If I have learnt anything, it is that life forms no logical patterns. It is haphazard and full of beauties which I try to catch as they fly by, for who knows whether any of them will ever return?

Margot Fonteyn

How often are you worrying about the present moment? The present moment is usually all right. If you're worrying, you're either agonizing over the past which you should have forgotten long ago, or else you're apprehensive over the future which hasn't even come yet. We tend to skip over the present moment which is the only moment God gives any of us to live.

Peace Pilgrim

I have always felt that the moment when first you wake up in the morning is the most wonderful of the twenty-four hours.

Monica Baldwin

"Now" is the operative word. Everything you put in your way is just a method of putting off the hour when you could actually be doing your dream. You don't need endless time and perfect conditions. Do it now. Do it today. Do it for twenty minutes and watch your heart start beating.

Barbara Sher

I am no longer waiting for some stress to end, or a busy time to be over, or a crisis to solve so that I can finally be happy. I've stopped putting off happiness "til later" and am loving and living life to its fullest right now. So can you.

Rita Emmett

Eternity is not something that begins after you are dead. It's going on all the time. We are in it now.

Charlotte Perkins Gilman

Pride

Every time we start thinking we're the centre of the universe, the universe turns around and says with a slightly distracted air, "I'm sorry. What'd you say your name was again?"

Margaret Maron

Proud people breed sad sorrows for themselves.
Emily Bronte

Nothing is easier than self-deceit. For what each man [person] wishes, that he [she] also believes to be true.

Diane Arbus

Problem Solving

It's not a problem that we have a problem. It's a problem if we don't deal with the problem.

Mary Kay Utech

There are two ways of meeting difficulties: You alter the difficulties or you alter yourself to meet them.

Phyllis Bottome

Ah, mastery... what a profoundly satisfying feeling when one finally gets on top of a new set of skills... and then sees the light under the new door those skills can open, even as another door is closing.

Gail Sheehy

Some problems cannot be solved but you can make peace with them.

Sanya Friedman

You have to ask the questions and attempt to find answers, because you're right in the middle of it; they've put you in charge – and during a hurricane too.

Sheila Ballantyne

If you can't solve it, it's not a problem – it's reality.

Barbara Colorose

Procrastination

To think too long about doing a thing often becomes its undoing.

Eva Young

A year from now you may wish you had started today.

Karen Lamb

Procrastination is my sin.
It brings me naught but sorrow.
I know that I should stop it.
In fact, I will – tomorrow!

Gloria Pitzer

Procrastination gives you something to look forward to.

Joan Konner

> When a man does a household job, he goes through three periods: contemplating how it will be done; contemplating when it will be done; and contemplating.
>
> *Marcelene Cox*

Don't fool yourself that important things can be put off till tomorrow; they can be put off forever, or not at all.

Mignon McLaughlin

All things come to those who wait, but when they come they're out of date.

Author unknown

Progress

Idealists… foolish enough to throw caution to the winds… have advanced mankind and have enriched the world.

Emma Goldman

Modern invention has banished the spinning wheel, and the same law of progress makes the woman of today a different woman from her grandmother.

Susan B. Anthony

> Progress everywhere today does seem to come so very heavily disguised as Chaos.
>
> *Joyce Grenfell*

You don't make progress by standing on the sidelines, whimpering and complaining. You make progress by implementing ideas.

Shirley Anita Chisholm

I was taught that the way of progress is neither swift nor easy.

Madame Marie Curie

I am suffocated and lost when I have not the bright feeling of progression.

Margaret Fuller

Most people are in favour of progress, it's the changes they don't like.

Author unknown

You just don't luck into things as much as you'd like to think you do. You build step by step, whether it's friendships or opportunities.

Barbara Bush

Woman must not accept; she must challenge. She must not be awed by that which has been built up around her; she must reverence that woman in her which struggles for expression.

Margaret Sanger

Purpose

The only failure a man ought to fear is failure in cleaving to the purpose he sees to be best.

George Eliot

Blessed are the single-hearted, for they shall enjoy much peace. If you refuse to be hurried and pressed, if you stay your soul on God, nothing can keep you from that clearness of spirit which is life and peace. In that stillness you will know what His will is.

Amy Carmichael

What allows us, as human beings, to psychologically survive life on earth, with all of its pain, drama and challenges, is a sense of purpose and meaning.

Barbara De Angelis

You can come to understand your purpose in life by slowing down and feeling your heart's desires.

Marcia Wieder

I think that a lot of women are made to feel that they have not done the one thing that they were put on the earth to do if they didn't do the normal thing, if they didn't take the most travelled path. And it's unfortunate.

Nanci Griffith

The presence of a long-term, conscious goal has helped me maintain stability through the ubiquitous changes of over half a century.

Mary Craig

I began to have an idea of my life, not as the slow shaping of achievement to fit my preconceived purposes, but as the gradual discovery and growth of a purpose which I did not know.

Joanna Field

R

Reading

A book burrows into your life in a very profound way because the experience of reading is not passive.

Erica Jong

Each time we re-read a book we get more out of it because we put more into it; a different person is reading it, and therefore it is a different book.

Murial Clark

Reading a book is like re-writing it for yourself. You bring to a novel, anything you read, all your experience of the world. You bring your history and you read it in your own terms.

Angela Carter

Reading makes immigrants of us all. It takes us away from home, but more important, it finds homes for us everywhere.

Hazel Rochman

We read books to find out who we are.

Dr Christine Northrup

A house is not a home unless it contains food and fire for the mind as well as the body.

Margaret Fuller

Just the knowledge that a good book is awaiting one at the end of a long day makes that day happier.

Kathleen Norias

The lessons taught in great books are misleading. The commerce in life is rarely so simple and never so just.

Anita Brookner

No story is the same to us after a lapse of time; or rather we who read it are no longer the same interpreters.

George Eliot

The pleasure of all reading is doubled when one lives with another who shares the same books.

Katherine Mansfield

Reality

What we call reality is an agreement that people have arrived at to make life more liveable.

Louise Nevelson

Every time I close the door on reality it comes in through the windows.

Jennifer Yane

The world is nothing but my perception of it. I see only through myself. I hear only through the filter of my story.

Byron Katie

The paradox of reality is that no image is as compelling as the one which exists only in the mind's eye.

Shana Alexander

Reality is something you rise above.

Liza Minnelli

I made some studies, and reality is the leading cause of stress amongst those in touch with it. I can take it in small doses, but as a lifestyle I found it too confining.

Jane Wagner

There are intangible realities which float near us, formless and without words; realities which no one has thought out, and which are excluded for lack of interpreters.

Natalie Clifford Barney

What is meant by reality? It would seem to be something very erratic, very undependable – now to be found in a dusty road, now in a scrap of newspaper in the street, now a daffodil in the sun.

Virginia Woolf

Regret

The follies that a person regrets most in his life are those which he didn't commit when he had an opportunity.

Helen Rowland

I have no regrets, I wouldn't have lived my life the way I did if I was going to worry about what people were going to say.

Ingrid Bergman

I have many regrets, and I'm sure everyone does. The stupid things you do, you regret if you have any sense, and if you don't regret them, maybe you're stupid.

Katharine Hepburn

Do you really want to look back on your life and see how wonderful it could have been had you not been afraid to live it.

Caroline Myss

I really don't think life is about the I-could-have-beens. Life is only about the I-tried-to-do. I don't mind the failure but I can't imagine that I'd forgive myself if I didn't try.

Nikki Giovanni

One doesn't recognize the really important moments in one's life until it's too late.

Agatha Christie

But penance need not be paid in suffering... It can be paid in forward motion. Correcting the mistake is a positive move, a nurturing move.

Barbara Hall

People have to face regrets. Becoming mature means learning to accept what you cannot change, facing unresolved sorrows and learning to love life as it really happens, not as you would have it happen. When your day's not perfect, it's not a failure or a terrible loss. It's just another day.

Barbara Sher

Relationships

If I had a single flower for every time I think about you, I could walk forever in my garden.

Claudia Ghandi

In nine cases out of ten, a woman had better show more affection than she feels.

Jane Austen

This has to be one of the best singles ads ever printed. It is reported to have been listed in the *Atlanta Journal*.

> SINGLE BLACK FEMALE seeks male companionship, ethnicity unimportant. I'm a very good girl who LOVES to play. I love long walks in the woods, riding in your pickup truck, hunting, camping and fishing trips, cosy winter nights lying by the fire. Candlelight dinners will have me eating out of your hand. I'll be at the front door when you get home from work, wearing only what nature gave me. Call (404) 875-6420 and ask for Daisy, I'll be waiting...

Over 15,000 men found themselves talking to the Atlanta Humane Society for Dogs.

Love has nothing to do with what you are expecting to get – only what you are expecting to give – which is everything. What you will receive in return varies. But it really has no connection with what you give. You give because you love and cannot help giving.

Katharine Hepburn

Love is the only thing that we can carry with us when we go, and it makes the end so easy.

Louisa May Alcott

We come to love not by finding the perfect person, but by learning to see an imperfect person perfectly.

Angelina Jolie

Intimacy is being seen and known as the person you truly are.

Amy Bloom

Love – a wildly misunderstood although highly desirable malfunction of the heart which weakens the brain, causes eyes to sparkle, cheeks to glow, blood pressure to rise and the lips to pucker.

Author unknown

Love, I find, is like singing. Everyone can do enough to satisfy themselves, though it may not impress the neighbours as being very much.

Zora Neale Hurtson

A woman's heart should be so hidden in Christ that a man should have to seek Him first to find her.

Maya Angelou

Love comes when manipulation stops; when you think more about the other person than about his or her reactions to you. When you dare to reveal yourself fully. When you dare to be vulnerable.

Dr. Joyce Brothers

Infatuation is when you think he's as sexy as Robert Redford, as smart as Henry Kissinger, as noble as Ralph Nader, as funny as Woody Allen and as athletic as Jimmy Conners. Love is when you realize that he's as sexy as Woody Allen, as smart as Jimmy Connors, as funny as Ralph Nader, as athletic as Henry Kissinger and nothing like Robert Redford – but you'll take him anyway.

Judith Viorst

When you realize you want to spend the rest of your life with somebody, you want the rest of your life to start as soon as possible.

Nora Ephron

Responsibility

Nothing strengthens the judgment and quickens the conscience like individual responsibility.

Elizabeth Cady Stanton

You cannot hope to build a better world without improving the individuals. To that end each of us must work for their own improvement and at the same time share a general responsibility for all humanity, our particular duty being to aid those to whom we think we can be most useful.

Marie Curie

The willingness to accept responsibility for one's own life is the source from which self-respect springs.

Joan Didion

As novices, we think we're entirely responsible for the way people treat us. I have long since learned that we are responsible only for the way we treat people.

Rose Wilder Lane

Each of us has the right and the responsibility to asses the road which lies ahead and those over which we have travelled, and if the future road looms ominous or unpromising, and the road back uninviting, then we need to gather our resolve and, carrying only the necessary baggage, step off that road into another direction. If the new choice is also unpalatable, without embarrassment, we must be ready to change that one as well.

Maya Angelou

I don't see the point of being a human being if you're not going to be responsible to your fellow human beings. Selfishness thefts away the human and reduces you to just a being.

Candea Core-Starke

Revolution

No one makes a revolution by himself; and there are some revolutions which humanity accomplishes without quite knowing how, because it is everybody who takes them in hand.

George Sand

Revolutions are notorious for allowing even non-participants – even women! – new scope for telling the truth since they are themselves such massive moments of truth, moments of such massive participation.

Selma James

In rebellion alone, woman is at ease, stamping out both prejudices and sufferings; all intellectual women will sooner or later rise in rebellion.

Louise Mitchell

The children of the revolution are always ungrateful, and the revolution must be grateful that it is so.

Ursula Le Guin

If a man has lived in a tradition which tells him that nothing can be done about his human condition, to believe that progress is possible may well be the greatest revolution of all.

Barbara Ward

To be a revolutionary you have to be a human being. You have to care about people who have no power.

Jane Fonda

Revolution begins with the self, in the self.

Toni Cade Bambara

True revolutionaries are like God – they create the world in their own image. Our awesome responsibility to ourselves, to our children and to the future is to create ourselves in the image of goodness, because the future depends on the nobility of our imaginings.

Barbara Grizzuli Harrison

Every successful revolution puts on in time the robes of the tyrant it has deposed.

Barbara Tuchman

It is time for women of biblical faith to reclaim our territory. We know the Designer. We have His instruction manual. If we don't display the Divine design of His female creation, no one will. But if we do, it will be a profound testimony to a watching, needy world.

Susan Hunt

Risk

When you play it too safe, you're taking the biggest risk of your life. Time is the only wealth we're given.

Barbara Sher

It's good to have a comfort zone, but you also have to push yourself.

Kathleen Brown

Life is a risk.
Diane Von Furstenberg

If you're never scared or embarrassed or hurt, it means you never take any chances.

Julia Sorel

It's better to be boldly decisive and risk being wrong than to agonize at length and be right too late.

Marilyn Moats Kennedy

Courageous risks are life-giving, they help you grow, make you brave, and better than you think you are.

Joan L. Curcio

Most people live and die with their music still unplayed. They never dare to try.

Mary Kay Ash

Perseverance and audacity generally win!

Madame Dorothe Deluzy

If you try to guard yourself against every unlikely danger, you'll never stretch beyond your comfort zone.

Diane Conway

If you play it safe in life, you've decided that you don't want to grow anymore.

Shirley Hufstedler

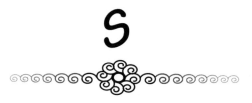

S

Sacrifice

There is no moral authority like that of sacrifice.

Nadine Gordimer

Life brings with it a cross shaped dimension which we have to bear whether we like it or not.

Rev Dr Liz Culling

My memory of convent-school Lents is actually rather satisfying: you give up a few pleasures, reacquaint yourself with mild hunger, remind your body that it is there to serve, not dominate, you, and make space for reflection, only occasionally dreaming of chocolate eggs to come.

Libby Purves

He who never sacrificed a present to a future good or a personal to a general one can speak of happiness only as the blind do of colours.

Olympia Brown

Self-sacrifice which denies common sense is not a virtue. It's a spiritual dissipation.

Margaret Deland

Security

Security is mostly a superstition. It does not exist in nature, nor do the children of men as a whole experience it. Avoiding danger is no safer in the long run than outright exposure. Life is either a daring adventure, or nothing.

Helen Keller

Security is when I'm very much in love with somebody extraordinary who loves me back.

Shelley Winters

There is no such thing as security. There never has been. Probably the only place where a man can feel really secure is in a maximum security prison, except for the imminent threat of release.

Germaine Greer

Only in growth, reform and change, paradoxically enough, is true security to be found.

Anne Morrow Lindbergh

> God himself is not secure, having given man dominion over his work.
>
> *Helen Keller*

Oh, the comfort, the inexpressible comfort of feeling safe with a person, having neither to weigh thoughts nor measure words, but pouring them all out, just as they are, chaff and grain together, certain that a faithful hand will take and sift them, keep what is worth keeping, and with a breath of kindness blow the rest away.

Dinah Craik

Self

I was right not to be afraid of any thief but myself, who will end by leaving me nothing.

Katherine Anne Porter

How much you value and accept yourself is central to every decision you make. If you feel you are not acceptable to yourself or other people, if you set yourself impossible standards and judge yourself too harshly, you make poor decisions and you suffer.

Dr Dorothy Rowe

I think your self emerges more clearly over time.

Meryl Streep

You are unique, and if that is not fulfilled then something has been lost.

Martha Graham

With fame, you know, you can read about yourself, somebody else's ideas about you, but what's important is how you feel about yourself – for survival and living day to day with what comes up.

Marilyn Monroe

What the world needs now is for each of us to be who we truly are, and to bring our gifts into the world. Don't hold back any longer. Be Present, Be You. That is enough. Really it is.

Nancy Bishop

Self-confidence

You can stand tall without standing on someone. You can be a victor without having victims.

Harriet Woods

The thing that is really hard, and really amazing, is giving up on being perfect and beginning the work of becoming yourself.

Anna Quindlen

If you're able to be yourself, then you have no competition. All you have to do is get closer and closer to that essence.

Barbara Cook

Why is it that only girls stand on the sides of their feet? As if they're afraid to plant themselves?

Barbara Kingsolver

Remove those 'I want you to like me' stickers from your forehead and, instead, place them where they truly will do the most good – on your mirror!

Susan Jeffers

Self-esteem

You're not what you think you are; you're not what others think you are; you're what you think others think you are!

Author unknown

Until you make peace with who you are, you'll never be content with what you have.

Doris Mortman

I am as my Creator made me and since He is satisfied, so am I.

Minnie Smith

Women who set a low value on themselves make life hard for all women.

Nellie McClung

Set your own value – and mean it.

Julie Schoenfeld

A person's worth is contingent upon who he is, not upon what he does, or how much he has. The worth of a person, or a thing, or an idea, is in being, not in doing, not in having.

Alice Mary Hilton

Self-esteem must be earned! When you dare to dream, dare to follow that dream, dare to suffer through the pain, sacrifice, self-doubts, and friction from the world, you will genuinely impress yourself.

Laura Schlessinger

Self-knowledge

There is a great deal of unmapped country within us which would have to be taken into account in an explanation of our gusts and storms.

George Eliot

When your heart speaks, take good notes.

Judith Campbell

You cannot fully understand your own life without knowing and thinking beyond your life, your own neighbourhood, and even your own nation.

Johnnetta Cole

There's a period of life when we swallow a knowledge of ourselves and it becomes either good or sour inside.

Pearl Bailey

Like an old gold-panning prospector, you must resign yourself to digging up a lot of sand from which you will later patiently wash out a few minute particles of gold ore.

Dorothy Bryant

There is an eternal landscape, a geography of the soul; we search for its outlines all our lives.

Josephine Hart

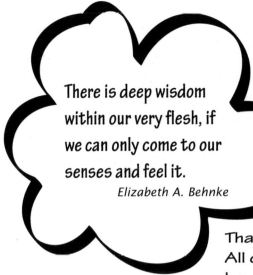

There is deep wisdom within our very flesh, if we can only come to our senses and feel it.

Elizabeth A. Behnke

God, why do I storm heaven for answers that are already in my heart? Every grace I need has already been given me. Oh, lead me to the Beyond within.

Macrina Wieherkehr

That's the way things come clear. All of a sudden. And then you realize how obvious they've been all along.

Madeleine L'Engle

After a deep inner search, I realized that we are programmed and tend to follow patterns of our past experiences without realizing what we are doing.

Hilary Cutler

Self-pity

There are few human emotions as warm, comforting and enveloping as self-pity. And nothing is more corrosive and destructive. There is only one answer; turn away from it and move on.

Dr Megan Reik

I've never been one to sit around and eat my heart out. Life's too short.

Kate Adie

Self-pity in its early stages is as snug as a feather mattress. Only when it hardens does it become uncomfortable.

Maya Angelou

She who is wrapped up in herself makes a mighty small package.

Author unknown

Self-pity is our worst enemy and if we yield to it, we can never do anything wise in the world.

Helen Keller

Never feel self-pity, the most destructive emotion there is. How awful to be caught up in the terrible squirrel cage of self.

Millicent Fenwick

Service

Everyone has the potential to give something back.

Diana, Princess of Wales

The only thing you will take through those pearly gates is what you have given away.

Marcia Moore

Service is the rent we pay for being. It is the very purpose of life, and not something you do in your spare time.

Marian Wright Edelman

To serve is beautiful, but only if it is done with joy and a whole heart and a free mind.

Pearl S. Buck

One's life has value so long as one attributes value to the life of others, by means of love, friendship, indignation and compassion.

Simone de Beauvoir

Sow good services: sweet remembrances will grow from them.

Germaine de Staël

You cannot hope to build a better world without improving the individuals. To that end, each of us must work for our own improvement and, at the same time, share a general responsibility for all humanity, our particular duty being to aid those to whom we think we can be most useful.

Marie Curie

Shopping

Ever notice that Soup For One is eight aisles away from Party Mix?

Elayne Boosler

Buying is a profound pleasure.

Simone de Beauvoir

The quickest way to know a woman is to go shopping with her.

Marcelene Cox

The woman just ahead of you at the supermarket checkout has all the delectable groceries you didn't even know they carried.

Mignon McLaughlin

The odds of going to the store for a loaf of bread and coming out with ONLY a loaf of bread are three billion to one.

Author unknown

Silence

Silence is the secret to sanity.

Astrid Alauda

Every day silence harvests its victims. Silence is a mortal illness.

Natalia Ginzberg

Learn to get in touch with the silence within yourself and know that everything in this life has a purpose.

Elisabeth Kubler-Ross

Silences make the real conversations between friends. Not the saying but the never needing to say is what counts.

Margaret Lee Runbeck

The deepest feeling always shows itself in silence.

Marianne Moore

Silence is more musical than any song.

Christina Rossetti

We need to find God, and he cannot be found in noise and restlessness. God is the friend of silence. See how nature – trees, flowers, grass – grows in silence; see the stars, the moon and the sun, how they move in silence… We need silence to be able to touch souls.

Mother Teresa

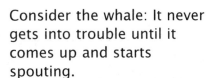

Consider the whale: It never gets into trouble until it comes up and starts spouting.

Author unknown

Silence is a sounding thing, to one who listens hungrily.

Gwendolyn Bennett

Simplicity

Simplicity is the most difficult thing to secure in this world; it is the last limit of experience and the last effort of genius.

George Sand

The trouble with simple living is that, though it can be joyful, rich and creative, it isn't simple.

Doris Janzen Longacre

The simplification of life is one of the steps to inner peace. A persistent simplification will create an inner and outer well-being that places harmony in one's life.

Peace Pilgrim

Frugality is one of the most beautiful and joyful words in the English language, and yet one that we are culturally cut off from understanding and enjoying. The consumption society has made us feel that happiness lies in having things, and has failed to teach us the happiness of not having things.

Elise Boulding

If you cultivate a healthy poverty and simplicity, so that finding a penny will literally make your day, then, since the world is in fact planted in pennies, you have with your poverty bought a lifetime of days.

Annie Dillard

I have learned by some experience… [that] certain modes of life, certain rules of conduct are more conducive to inner and outer harmony than others. There are, in fact, certain roads that one may follow. Simplification of life is one of them.

Ann Morrow Lindbergh

Solitude

There are days when solitude is a heady wine that intoxicates you with freedom, others when it is a bitter tonic and still others when it is a poison that makes you beat your head against the wall.

Sidonie-Gabrielle Colette

Solitude is the human condition in which I keep myself company. Loneliness comes about when I am alone without being able to split up into the two-in-one, without being able to keep myself company.

Hannah Arendt

Isolation is aloneness that feels forced upon you, like a punishment. Solitude is aloneness you choose and embrace. I think great things can come out of solitude, out of going to a place where all is quiet except the beating of your heart.

Jeanne Marie Laskas

I admire people who are suited to the contemplative life... They can sit inside themselves like honey in a jar and just be. It's wonderful to have someone like that around; you always feel you can count on them.

Elizabeth Janeway

Solitude is such a potential thing. We hear voices in solitude, we never hear in the hurry and turmoil of life; we receive counsels and comforts, we get under no other condition.

Amelia Barr

Being solitary is being alone well: being alone luxuriously immersed in doings of your own choice, aware of the fullness of your own presence rather than of the absence of others – because solitude is an achievement.

Alice Koller

We in the developed world seem to have many auditory strategies that insulate us from the presence of silence, simplicity and solitude. When I return to Western culture after time in desert, mountain or forest, I discover how we have filled our world with a multiplicity of noises, a symphony of forgetfulness that keeps our own thoughts and realizations, feelings and intuitions out of audible range.

Joan Halifax

Inside myself is a place where I live all alone and that's where you renew your springs that never dry up.

Pearl S. Buck

Stress

Brent Bost, Texas gynaecologist, says that ['hurried woman syndrome'] affects women who have to juggle work, home and kids, and leaves them chronically stressed. This in turn kills their sex drive and leads to weight gain through comfort eating. They then feel guilty and suffer low self esteem... the cure, apparently, is to stop hurrying. That simple, huh?

Body & Soul Supplement, The Times, 8 January 2005

I try to take one day at a time, but sometimes several days attack me at once.

Jennifer Yane

Sometimes the most important thing in a whole day is the rest we take between two deep breaths.

Etty Hillesum

Stress is an ignorant state. It believes that everything is an emergency.

Natalie Goldberg

When I am at all hassled about something, I always stop and ask myself what difference it will make in the evolution of the human species in the next ten million years, and that question always helps me get back my perspective.

Anne Wilson Schaef

For fast-acting relief try slowing down.

Lily Tomlin

You don't get ulcers from what you eat. You get them from what's eating you.

Vicki Baum

Submission

If you surrender to the wind, you can ride it.

Toni Morrison

Only in proportion as our own will is surrendered are we able to discern the splendour of God's will.

Frances Havergal

Some think it's holding on that makes one strong; sometimes it's letting go.

Sylvia Robinson

When you relinquish the desire to control your future, you can have more happiness.

Nicole Kidman

Almighty and Eternal God, the Disposer of all the affairs in the world, there is not one circumstance so great as not to be subject to Thy power, nor so small but it comes within Thy care... may we readily submit ourselves to Thy pleasure and sincerely resign our wills to Thine, with all patience, meekness and humility.

Queen Anne

Obedience is really about love. It is our loving response to God which a murmuring response altogether wrecks.

Esther de Waal

Success

To follow without halt, one aim; there is the secret of success. And success? What is it? I do not find it in the applause of the theatre; it lies rather in the satisfaction of accomplishment.

Anna Pavlova

Success is having a flair for the thing that you are doing, knowing that is not enough, that you have got to have hard work and a sense of purpose.

Margaret Thatcher

The best thing that can come with success is the knowledge that it is nothing to long for.

Liv Ullman

The worst part of success is to try to find someone who is happy for you.

Bette Midler

Success can make you go one of two ways. It can make you a prima donna, or it can smooth the edges, take away the insecurities, let the nice things come out.

Barbara Walters

Even a stopped clock is right twice every day. After some years, it can boast of a long series of successes.

Marie Von Ebner-Eschenbach

Women share with men the need for personal success, even the taste of power, and no longer are we willing to satisfy those needs through the achievements of surrogates, whether husbands, children or merely role models.

Elizabeth Dole

Success supposes
endeavour.

Jane Austen

Success
breeds
confidence.

Beryl Markham

Generally speaking, we are all
happier when we are still
striving for achievement than
when the prize is in our hands.

Margot Fonteyn

Success does not implant bad
characteristics in people. It
merely steps up the growth rate
of the bad characteristics they
already had.

Margaret Halsey

I find it's as hard to live
down an early triumph
as an early indiscretion.

Edna St Vincent Millay

It isn't success
after all, is it, if it
isn't an expression
of your deepest
energies?

Marilyn French

What does
so-called success
or failure matter if
only you have
succeeded in doing
the thing you set
out to do. The
DOING is all that
really counts.

Eva Le Gallienne

Success is a two-bladed golden
sword; it knights one and stabs
one at the same time.

Mae West

Suffering

Although the world is full of suffering, it is full also of the overcoming of it.

Helen Keller

Pain is inevitable. Suffering is optional.

M. Kathleen Casey

It is not suffering as such that is most deeply feared but suffering that degrades.

Susan Sontag

When the Japanese mend broken objects, they aggrandize the damage by filling the cracks with gold. They believe that when something's suffered damage and has a history it becomes more beautiful.

Barbara Bloom

To live is to suffer, to survive is to find some meaning in the suffering.

Roberta Flack

Don't cry when the sun is gone, because the tears won't let you see the stars.

Violeta Parra

One must really have suffered oneself to help others.

Mother Teresa

T

Talent

There are two kinds of talent, man-made talent and God-given talent. With man-made talent you have to work very hard. With God-given talent, you just touch it up once in a while.

Pearl Bailey

The only thing that happens overnight is recognition. Not talent.

Carol Haney

We can't take any credit for our talents. It's how we use them that counts.

Madeleine L'Engle

Patience is an integral part of talent.

Vicki Baum

It is one thing to be gifted and quite another thing to be worthy of one's own gift.

Nadia Boulanger

A career is born in public – talent in privacy.

Marilyn Monroe

We do not know and cannot tell when the spirit is with us. Great talent or small, it makes no difference. We are caught within our own skins, our own sensibilities; we never know if our technique has been adequate to the vision.

Madeleine L'Engle

Talent, like beauty, to be pardoned, must be obscure and unostentatious.

Lady Marguerite Blessington

Teenagers

The invention of the teenager was a mistake. Once you identify a period of life in which people get to stay out late but don't have to pay taxes – naturally, no one wants to live any other way.

Judith Martin

Adolescence is perhaps nature's way of preparing parents to welcome the empty nest.

Karen Savage and Patricia Adams

You can tell a child is growing up when he stops asking where he came from and starts refusing to tell where he is going.

Author unknown

It's difficult to decide whether growing pains are something teenagers have – or are.

Author unknown

What a shame that allowances have to stop with the teens: both those that are paid to us and those that are made for us.

Mignon McLaughlin

The troubles of adolescence eventually all go away –
it's just like a really long, bad cold.

Dawn Ruelas

Small children disturb your sleep, big children your life.

Yiddish proverb

How strange that the young should always think the world is against them – when in fact that is the only time it is for them?

Mignon McLaughlin

I have seen my kid struggle into the kitchen in the morning wearing outfits that need only one accessory: an empty gin bottle.

Erma Bombeck

At fourteen you don't need sickness or death for tragedy.

Jessamyn West

As a teenager you are at the last stage in your life when you will be happy to hear that the phone is for you.

Fran Lebowitz

Adolescents are not monsters. They are just people trying to learn how to make it among the adults in the world, who are probably not so sure themselves.

Virginia Satir

Helping your eldest to pick a college is one of the greatest educational experiences of life – for the parents. Next to trying to pick his bride, it's the best way to learn that your authority, if not entirely gone, is slipping fast.

Sally and James Reston

Temptation

Temptations come, as a general rule, when they are sought.

Margaret Oliphant

The virtue which has never been attacked by temptation is deserving of no monument.

Mademoiselle Madeleine de Scuderi

Temptations, like misfortunes, are sent to test our moral strength.

Marguerite de Valois

The time for reasoning is before we have approached near enough to the forbidden fruit to look at it and admire.

Margaret Percival

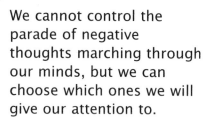

We cannot control the parade of negative thoughts marching through our minds, but we can choose which ones we will give our attention to.

Gladys Edmunds

No temptation can ever be measured by the value of its object.

Sidonie-Gabrielle Colette

Opportunity may knock only once, but temptation leans on the doorbell.

Author unknown

Life is very difficult. It seems right to me sometimes that we should follow our strongest feelings; but then such feelings continually come across the ties that all our former life has made for us – the ties that have made others dependent on us – and would cut them in two.

George Eliot

Thinking

The truth is that thinking like a woman can be a tremendous advantage.

Mary Kay Ash

Thoughts have power. Thoughts are energy. And you can make your world or break your world by your thinking.

Susan L. Taylor

To think and to be fully alive are the same.
Hannah Arendt

If you want your life to be rewarding you have to change to way you think.

Oprah Winfrey

There are no dangerous thoughts; thinking itself is dangerous.

Hannah Arendt

You live with your thoughts – so be careful what they are.

Eva Arrington

I refuse the compliment that I think like a man, thought has no sex, one either thinks or one does not.

Clare Boothe Luce

The trouble with most people is that they think with their hopes or fears or wishes rather than their minds.

Nancy Astor

Time

Time is a fixed income and, as with any income, the real problem facing most of us is how to live successfully within our daily allotment.

Margaret B. Johnstone

If you realize too acutely how valuable time is, you are too paralyzed to do anything.

Katharine Hathaway

Time, when it is left to itself and no definite demands are made on it, cannot be trusted to move at any recognized pace. Usually it loiters; but just when one has come to count upon its slowness, it may suddenly break into a wild irrational gallop.

Edith Wharton

Let not the sands of time get in your lunch.

Author unknown

Time is a great healer, but a poor beautician.

Lucille S.Harper

All my possessions for a moment of time.

Queen Elizabeth I

One must learn a different... sense of time, one that depends more on small amounts than big ones.

Sister Mary Paul

Tradition

Traditions are the guideposts driven deep in our subconscious minds. The most powerful ones are those we can't even describe and aren't even aware of.

Ellen Goodman

Old-fashioned ways which no longer apply to changed conditions are a snare in which the feet of women have always become readily entangled.

Jane Addams

Custom is the tyranny of the lower human faculties over the higher.

Madame Suzanne Curchod Necker

No written law has ever been more binding than unwritten custom supported by popular opinion.

Carrie Chapman Catt

People do more from custom than from reason.

Author unknown

Old habits are strong and jealous.

Dorothea Brande

Tradition! We scarcely know the word anymore. We are afraid to be either proud of our ancestors or ashamed of them.

Dorothy Day

The bird that would soar above the plain of tradition and prejudice must have strong wings.

Kate Chopin

Travel

The true fruit of travel is perhaps the feeling of being nearly everywhere at home.

Freya Stark

To me travel is a triple delight: anticipation, performance and recollection.

Ilka Chase

Travelling is the ruin of all happiness! There's no looking at a building here after seeing Italy.

Fanny Burney

I am never happier than when I am alone in a foreign city; it is as if I had become invisible.

Storm Jameson

Through travel I first became aware of the outside world; it was through travel that I found my own introspective way into becoming a part of it.

Eudora Welty

One should learn patience in a foreign land, for… this is the true measure of travel. If one does not suffer some frustration of the ordinary reflexes, how can one be sure one is really travelling?

Gertrude Diamant

Loving life is easy when you are abroad. Where no one knows you and you hold your life in your hands all alone, you are more master of yourself than at any other time.

Hannah Arendt

The true traveller is he who goes on foot, and even then, he sits down a lot of the time.

Sidonie-Gabrielle Colette

I have learned this strange thing, too, about travel: one may return to a place and, quite unexpectedly, meet oneself still lingering there from the last time.

Helen Bevington

Surely one advantage of travelling is that, while it removes much prejudice against foreigners and their customs, it intensifies tenfold one's appreciation of the good at home.

Isabella L. Bird

When travelling abroad if you see something you yearn for, if you can afford it at all, buy it. If you don't you'll regret it all your life.

Ilka Chase

The impulse to travel is one of the hopeful symptoms of life.

Agnes Repplier

A trip is what you take when you can't take any more of what you've been taking.
Adeline Ainsworth

Trips do not end when you return home – usually this is the time when in a sense they really begin.

Agnes E. Benedict and Adele Franklin

Trust

I could be whatever I wanted to be if I trusted that music, that song, that vibration of God that was inside of me.

Shirley MacLaine

Even now, I find that no matter what has happened, I still have that trust. I have a lot of trust, that people can be better than they are.

Alice Walker

Foolish are they indeed who trust to fortune!

Lady Murasaki

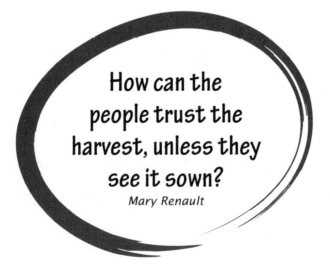

How can the people trust the harvest, unless they see it sown?
Mary Renault

Allies never trust each other, but that doesn't spoil their effectiveness.

Ayn Rand

He who has trusted where he ought not will surely mistrust where he ought not.

Marie Von Ebner-Eschenbach

Those who trust us, educate us.

George Eliot

Trust, which is a virtue, is also a habit, like prayer. It requires exercise. And just as no one can run five miles a day and cede the cardiovascular effects to someone else, no one can trust for us.

Sue Halpern

Truth

The important thing is not the finding, it is the seeking, it is the devotion with which one spins the wheel of prayer and scripture, discovering the truth little by little. If this machine gave you the truth immediately, you would not recognize it.

Ursula Le Guin

The truth is the kindest thing we can give folks in the end.

Harriet Beecher Stowe

Truth isn't always beauty, but the hunger for it is.

Nadine Gordimer

The truth comes out in jokes.

Vicki Marsala

Marvellous Truth, confront us at every turn, in every guise.

Denise Levertov

The trouble about man is twofold. He cannot learn truths which are too complicated; he forgets truths which are too simple.

Rebecca West

When a woman tells the truth she is creating the possibility for more truth around her.

Adrienne Rich

Funny how people despise platitudes, when they are usually the truest thing going. A thing has to be pretty true before it gets to be a platitude.

Katherine F.Gerould

You never find yourself until you face the truth.

Pearl Bailey

The best mind-altering drug is truth.

Lily Tomlin

If you *do* not tell the truth about yourself you cannot tell it about other people.

Virginia Woolf

U

Understanding

The crown of life is neither happiness nor annihilation; it is understanding.

Winifred Holtby

> ## Those who understand only what can be explained understand very little.
> *Marie von Ebner-Eschenbach*

The motto should not be: Forgive one another; rather, Understand one another.

Emma Goldman

More piercing, more unbearable than blame, is to be understood.

Frances Cornford

If you can keep your head when all about you are losing theirs, it's just possible you haven't grasped the situation.

Jean Kerr

Nothing's easier than believing we understand experiences we've never had.

Gwen Bristow

People don't want to be understood – I mean not completely. It's too destructive. Then they haven't anything left. They don't want complete sympathy or complete understanding. They want to be treated carelessly and taken for granted lots of times.

Anne Morrow Lindbergh

Whatever people in general do not understand, they are always prepared to dislike; the incomprehensible is always the obnoxious.

L.E. Landon

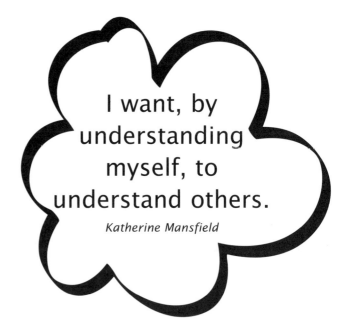

I want, by understanding myself, to understand others.

Katherine Mansfield

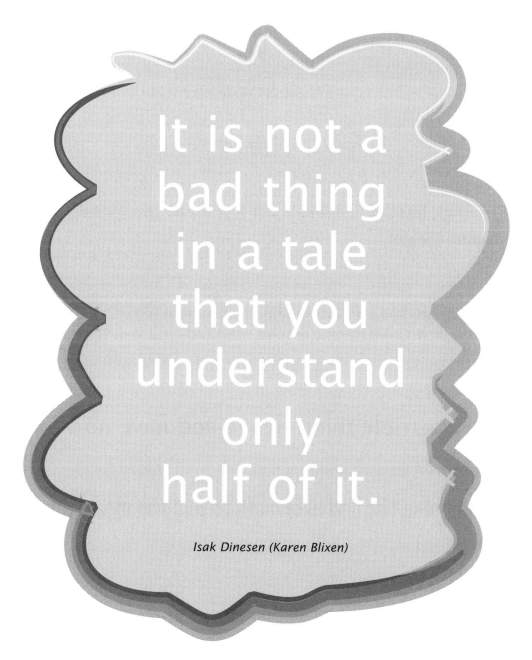

It is not a bad thing in a tale that you understand only half of it.

Isak Dinesen (Karen Blixen)

More piercing, more unbearable than blame
Is to be understood.

Frances Cornford

V

Vision

Reach high, for stars lie hidden in your soul. Dream deep, for every dream precedes the goal.

Pamela Vaull Starr

Throughout the centuries there were men who took first steps, down new roads, armed with nothing but their own vision.

Ayn Rand

It is a terrible thing to see and have no vision.

Helen Keller

Envisioning the end is enough to put the means in motion.

Dorothea Brande

For light I go directly to the Source of Light, not to any of the reflections.

Peace Pilgrim

A vision without a task is but a dream. A task without a vision is drudgery. A vision with a task is the hope of the world.

Author unknown

W

Wisdom

A wise woman puts a grain of sugar into everything she says to a man, and takes a grain of salt with everything he says to her.
Helen Rowland

Let us not take ourselves too seriously. None of us has a monopoly on wisdom.
Queen Elizabeth II

Only in the oasis of silence can we drink deeply from the inner cup of wisdom.
Sue Patton Thoele

Be happy. It's one way of being wise.
Sidonie-Gabrielle Colette

Silence and reserve will give anyone a reputation for wisdom.
Myrtle Reed

Wit

Wit consists in knowing the resemblance of things which differ, and the difference of things which are alike.

Madame de Staël

It is often a sign of wit not to show it, and not to see that others want it.

Madame Suzanne Curchod Necker

There's a hell of a distance between wise-cracking and wit. Wit has truth in it; wise-cracking is simply callisthenics with words.

Dorothy Rothchild Parker

People who can't be witty exert themselves to be devout and affectionate.

George Eliot

The more wit one has…the more one must remember not to use this weapon too freely, for the sharpest of swords make the most dangerous wounds.

Marie Adele Garnier

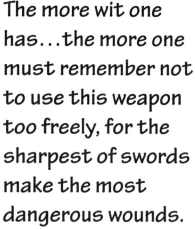

Wit is an intermittent fountain; kindness is a perennial spring.

Marie von Ebner-Eschenbach

Wealth

'Tis a sort of duty to be rich, that it may be in one's power to do good, riches being another word for power.

Lady Mary Wortley Montagu

It's just as bad being too rich as it is too tall. In the first case you can't find happiness. In the second case you can't find a bed.

Gabrielle "Coco" Chanel

There must be a reason why some people can afford to live well. They must have worked for it. I only feel angry when I see waste. When I see people throwing away things that we could use.

Mother Teresa

I'd rather have roses on my table than diamonds round my neck.

Emma Goldman

"Your money, or your life." We know what to do when a burglar makes this demand of us, but not when God does.

Mignon McLaughlin

There is a gigantic difference between earning a great deal of money and being rich.

Marlene Dietrich

Wealth is the product of man's capacity to think.

Ayn Rand

Women prefer men who have something tender about them – especially the legal kind.

Kay Ingram

Words

Words are less needful to sorrow than to joy.

Helen Hunt Jackson

Your own words are the bricks and mortar of the dreams you want to realize. Your words are the greatest power you have. The words you choose and their use establish the life you experience.

Sonia Croquette

Handle them carefully, for words have more power than atom bombs.

Pearl Strachan Hurd

The two most beautiful words in the English language are: Cheque Enclosed.

Dorothy Parker

Without words to objectify and categorize our sensations and place them in relation to one another, we cannot evolve a tradition of what is real in the world.

Ruth Hubbard

Kind words may be short... but their echoes are endless.

Mother Theresa

Words, words, words! says Hamlet, disparagingly. But God preserve us from the destructive power of words! There are words which can separate hearts sooner than sharp swords. There are words whose sting can remain through a whole life!

Mary Howitt

Women

I have always found women difficult. I don't really understand them. To begin with, few women tell the truth.

Barbara Cartland

Women are the only exploited group in history to have been idealized into powerlessness.

Erica Jong

They talk about a woman's sphere, as though it had a limit. There's not a place in earth or heaven. There's not a task to mankind given... without a woman in it.

Kate Field

Femininity appears to be one of those pivotal qualities that is so important no one can define it.

Caroline Bird

Some women work so hard to make good husbands that they forget to make good wives.

Author unknown

A complete woman is probably not a very admirable creature. She is manipulative, uses other people to get her own way, and works within whatever system she is in.

Anita Brookner

There is a special place in hell for women who do not help other women.

Madeleine K. Albright

If it weren't for women, men would still be
wearing last week's socks.
Cynthia Nelms

If Miss means
respectably unmarried,
and Mrs. respectably
married, then Ms.
means nudge, nudge,
wink, wink.

Angela Carter

A woman is the full circle.
Within her is the power to
create, nurture and
transform.

Diane Mariechild

The woman who can
create her own job is
the woman who will
win fame and fortune.

Amelia Earhart

Work

I learned the value of hard work by working hard.

Margaret Mead

Nothing will work unless you do.

Maya Angelou

To each man is reserved a work which he alone can do.

Susan Blow

If you have fun at your job you are going to be more effective.

Meg Whitman

There is always the danger that we may just do the work for the sake of the work. This is where the respect and the love and the devotion come in – that we do it to God, to Christ, and that's why we try to do it as beautifully as possible.

Mother Teresa

Work is and always has been my salvation and I thank the Lord for it.

Louisa May Alcott

Remember that your work comes only moment by moment, and as surely as God calls you to work, he gives the strength to do it.

Priscilla Maurice

A person who has not done one half his day's work by ten o clock, runs a chance of leaving the other half undone.

Emily Brontë

I think you should take your job seriously, but not yourself – that is the best combination.

Judy Dench

Laziness may appear attractive but work gives satisfaction.

Anne Frank

Worry

Anxiety is the rust of life, destroying its brightness and weakening its power. A childlike and abiding trust in Providence is its best preventive and remedy.

Author unknown

I keep the telephone of my mind open to peace, harmony, health, love and abundance. Then whenever doubt, anxiety or fear tries to call me, they keep getting a busy signal and soon they'll forget my number.

Edith Armstrong

Why worry?

40 per cent of my worries will never happen, for anxiety is the result of a tired mind.

30 per cent concern old decisions which cannot be altered.

12 per cent centre on criticisms, mostly untrue, made by people who feel inferior.

10 per cent are related to my health, which worsens as I worry.

And only 8 per cent are 'legitimate', showing that life does have real problems which may be met head on when I eliminate senseless worries.

Author unknown

Don't chain your worries to your body. The burden soon becomes heavy and your health will give too much of itself to pick up the extra load.

Astrid Alauda

Love looks forward, hate looks back, anxiety has eyes all over its head.

Mignon McLaughlin

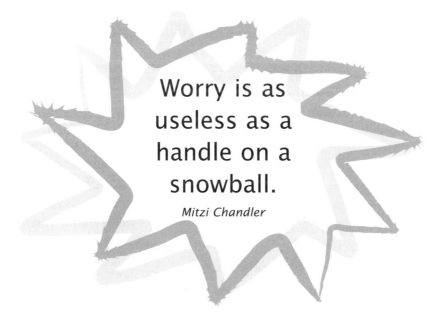

Worry is as useless as a handle on a snowball.

Mitzi Chandler

Worry is like a rocking chair – it gives you something to do but it doesn't get you anywhere.

Dorothy Galyean

Y

Youth

The young do not know enough to be prudent, and therefore they attempt the impossible – and achieve it, generation after generation.

Pearl S.Buck

Time misspent in youth is sometimes all the freedom one ever has.

Anita Brookner

Youth troubles over eternity, age grasps at a day and is satisfied to have even the day.

Dame Mary Gilmore

A youth with his first cigar makes himself sick; a youth with his first girl makes everybody sick.

Mary Little

There is nothing can pay one for that invaluable ignorance which is the companion of youth, those sanguine groundless hopes, and that lively vanity which makes all the happiness of life.

Lady Mary Wortley Montagu

Youth is not a time of life, it is a state of mind. You are as old as your doubt, your fear, your despair. The way to keep young is to keep your faith young. Keep your self-confidence young. Keep your hope young.

Luella F. Phean